$1

The Best
AUSTRALIAN POETRY
2005

THE BEST AUSTRALIAN POETRY SERIES

The Best Australian Poetry 2004
Guest Editor: Anthony Lawrence

The Best Australian Poetry 2003
Guest Editor: Martin Duwell

The Best
AUSTRALIAN POETRY
2005

Guest Editor
PETER PORTER

SERIES EDITORS
BRONWYN LEA & MARTIN DUWELL

First published 2005 by University of Queensland Press
Box 6042, St Lucia, Queensland 4067 Australia

www.uqp.uq.edu.au

Typeset in Times by Post Pre-Press Group, Brisbane, Queensland
Printed in Australia by McPherson's Printing Group

Distributed in the USA and Canada by
International Specialized Books Services, Inc.,
5824 N.E. Hassalo Street, Portland, Oregon 97213–3640

This project has been assisted by
the Commonwealth Government through
the Australia Council, its arts funding
and advisory body.

This publication is proudly sponsored by The Josephine Ulrick
and Win Schubert Foundation for the Arts.

Cover painting by Andrea Blackman, *Divine Lines*, 2004, Acrylic/Gouache/Canvas
(70 × 160 cm) courtesy of the artist and Art Galleries Schubert

Cataloguing in Publication Data
National Library of Australia

The best Australian poetry 2005.

   1. Australian poetry – 21st century – Collections.
   I. Duwell, Martin, 1948– . II. Lea, Bronwyn, 1969– .

A821.4

ISBN 0 7022 3518 0

CONTENTS

Hollits — ball

BRONWYN LEA AND MARTIN DUWELL

FOREWORD

One of the tasks of these series editors' forewords is to map (or, at least, to sketch) what has happened in Australian poetry in the year under review in the anthology. In previous anthologies this seems to have involved us lamenting the deaths of major poets and so there is a certain relief in discovering that this year has been one of few deaths. Sometimes it is good not to live in 'interesting times'. True, we have to mourn the closing of the journal *Salt-lick: New Poetry* – entirely devoted to poetry and thus responsible for publishing large numbers of poems, and good poems at that. And we note also the closing of Duffy & Snellgrove, which since 1996 has published books of poems by a number of Australia's finest poets, including three poets found in this year's anthology: Les Murray, Peter Goldsworthy and Stephen Edgar. Both these closures are indeed unfortunate, but we remain hopeful that new ventures will arise in their place.

One matter worth celebrating is the fact that the editor of this third anthology is one of the most distinguished poets writing in English. Peter Porter was born in Toowoomba, settled early in England, and over the last thirty years or so has renewed poetic contact with Australia to the point where he edited an important anthology of Australian poetry, *The Oxford Book of Modern Australian Verse*, in 1996. And he has been a regular revisitor ever since. He has also had a lot to do with the writing careers of a number of younger poets. He has proved to be a sympathetic mentor to these poets and has been a generous supporter of many others while at the same time keeping an eye on what is happening in poetry in Australia. So the perspective he provides in this anthology is animated not only by his own stature as a poet but by a genuine interest in the literary life of the country of his birth.

His most recent book, *Afterburner*, published by Picador in 2004 is the eighteenth in a book publishing career which began in 1961 with *Once Bitten, Twice Bitten*. As a poet, Porter has a reputation for metaphysical daring, an immersion in European culture, and an almost morbid fascination with death and dissolution. This reputation is not entirely undeserved but it is worth noting that he is also one of the wittiest poets ever to have written in English. Some of these interests are inevitably carried over into the selection he has made for this anthology. Many of the poems here derive from contemporary Australian poetry's renewed engagement with intellectual speculation.

Another feature of this selection, perhaps not out of keeping with this, is the number of long poems. The works of J.S. Harry, John Jenkins, John Kinsella and Fay Zwicky are all different kinds of long poems and exploit its different potentials. One is a surreal journey into a kind of Lewis Carroll-like environment in which philosophical positions can be looked at from an actualised perspective. The second is an imaginary meeting between a gangster and a great poet in a setting so associated with the poet that it seems like an externalisation of his mind (Stevens was, of course, obsessed by the relationship between the mind and reality and also with the nature of fictions). And the other two are more personal narratives distinguished by the fact that the former moves outward towards social documentation and the latter moves inward to register the effect of the alien on the young traveller. Then there are poems such as those by Chris Wallace-Crabbe and Geoffrey Lehmann which are extended works made up of individual units often providing different perspectives.

So it is good to see the long poem make a comeback of sorts. Generally Australia's poetic tradition has avoided both minimalism and really extended poems although the verse narrative did re-emerge in the 1980s in the work of John Scott, Alan Wearne, Les Murray and Dorothy Porter. Rereading John Tranter's important anthology of 1979, *The New Australian Poetry*, it is always a surprise to see how many long poems it contains: the twenty-two pages devoted to the work of Martin Johnston, for example, comprises two poems: 'The Blood Aquarium' and 'Microclimatology' and the whole of Robert Adamson's 'The Rumour' is included. Not only are there a high percentage of extended works but now, in retrospect, they seem to form the backbone of the collection.

Introducing the collection in this way, with an emphasis on its editor's preference for speculation over lyric celebration might be something of a misrepresentation. Many of the poems in this selection demonstrate a profound interest in the human sphere and it reminds us that Porter, in a recent lecture (republished in the *Australian Book Review*), has emphasised this contribution from the 'huge Commissariat of Poetry': 'We tend to think of poetry as descriptive, pastoral, lyrical or rhetorical – above all as lapidary, concerned with its own means, with language at unconsciousness's most intrinsic borders. But it would get nowhere without its human subjects, the material of social life, material closer to home than trees, cataracts or sublimities of Nature.'

GUEST EDITOR

PETER PORTER

Peter Porter has recently discovered that he is descended from one Christopher Porter, architect and builder, who was born in Nottingham, England in 1801 and emigrated to Geelong, with his family of ten children, in 1853. He and his eldest son, Robert, erected several buildings in Victoria, moving to Brisbane in 1860. Robert continued in the same profession and was Mayor of Brisbane in 1882. Losing his money, he died in 1902. Frederick his son and William his grandson kept the Porter line going in comparative penury. Peter (your editor), William's son, was born in a hospital in Kangaroo Point in 1929. He was educated at public schools in Brisbane and Toowoomba, leaving school in 1946. After training unsuccessfully as a journalist, he sailed to London in 1951, where he has lived ever since.

However, his long sojourn in England has been interrupted by many trips back to Australia, and he considers himself a citizen of both countries and affiliated to the literature of each. (He retains an Australian passport.) In the UK he has worked in bookselling and advertising, and has been for over thirty years a literary journalist and reviewer in London. His articles and poems have appeared in such journals as *The Times Literary Supplement*, *London Magazine*, *Encounter* (demised), *New Statesman*, *Poetry Review*, and *The Best Australian Poetry 2003*. His chief self-justification is his poetry. He has published sixteen volumes of verse, and collaborated in four books of poetry and graphics with the painter Arthur Boyd. His

Collected Poems, 1961–1999 (2 vols) was issued by Oxford University Press in 1999. Since then he has published two books of verse, *Max Is Missing* (Picador, 2001), which won the Forward Prize in 2002, and the recent collection *Afterburner*, 2004. He has edited several collections of poems and stories for the British Council and compiled *The Oxford Book of Modern Australian Verse* (1996). He is a frequent broadcaster on the BBC and ABC.

He won the Gold Medal of the Australian Literary Society in 1990; the Whitbread Poetry Prize, 1987; and was awarded the Queen's Gold Medal for Poetry, 2002. He is an Associate Fellow of the Australian Academy of the Humanities.

Peter Porter

Introduction

In an age of product labelling, it behoves an editor of such an anthology as this to offer a few observations about the concept 'Best'. Once you pass the number two, the comparative dissolves into a mass of superlatives. Indeed, the superlative becomes meaningless once it takes into account anything more than three. But this is to be over-scrupulous and mathematical. There are 130 pages of poems in this book, by forty poets. Reading them is an invitation to comparative, rather than superlative, judging. The anthology, as reiterated in its advertised description and described in the Series Editors' foreword, is compiled from poems written by poets of Australian nationality which have appeared during 2004 in Australian journals of all sorts. They are cumulatively 'the best' which I, as Guest Editor, could find in as wide an assortment of magazines as collated for me by the Series Editors. What Australian poets publish overseas and what foreign poets publish here is not eligible. Nevertheless, I have had an embarrassment of riches to cope with and have felt saddened at having to leave out work which was entirely worthy of inclusion. Space was not as restricting as number. I could not call the collection *The Better Australian Poetry 2005*: my use of the comparative in this introduction is just a more democratic way of justifying the selection I have made. Compared with the total of one year's production in journalistic publications – if a poem appeared in an author's book at the same time it would still be eligible if it received its first magazine appearance during the year – these, I believe, are the good stuff – I am happy to offer them as 'the best.'

One salient point which will strike a reader immediately is the preponderance of long poems. The contributions from J.S. Harry, John Jenkins, John Kinsella and Fay Zwicky take up half the book's space. I make no apology for this. These poems are among the most striking I have encountered anywhere recently. There is as much lapidary excellence of a line-by-line sort in their extended development as there is in any of the more concise pieces which make up the rest of the collection. Choosing these longer works is also an act of critical evolution. I have always wished for poetry to escape, if not the fact, then the editorial dominance, of the lyric, whether pastoral, anecdotal or cryptic. Years ago, when I was starting out, I was invited to address a university English department on some poetic topic, and chose as my title 'Doing Without the Lyric.' Naïve as I then was, I was developing a theme which has remained with me – how to claim back for poetry from prose some of its empowering scope and dramatic force. How, in fact, to revive that verse structure which is the glory of Augustan English, thing discursive essay or forensic argument – the sort of thing Alexander Pope achieved in his "Moral Essays' and epistles to his friends.

John Jenkins's 'Under the Shaded Blossom' is an extraordinary mixture of narrative and analysis, its subject close to the heart of American writers of the thirties. Noticing that the great poet Wallace Stevens was in Havana at the same time as a notorious New York mobster, Jenkins has the two meet and debate American, Cuban and dialectical morality in the bar of a Havana hotel. In its witty deployment of everyday language it might be one of Hemingway's laconic stories, but it is also a brilliant imposition on the real world of the metaphysical dimensions of Stevens's imagination. This is one of those rare works sophisticated enough to deserve the subheading 'post modern.'

Another over-used term might be fitted with more justice to J.S. Harry's 'Journeys West of "War"' – 'Surrealist.' Except that Harry's mind resolutely refuses such classification. Some years ago she adopted Peter Rebus (Rabbit) and set him on various journeys into the worlds of deceit, subterfuge and misrepresentation (these words are not synonyms). Her style is light and referential but the humour is severe and circumstantial. In his earlier adventures Peter was content to wander around Balmain and other Australian territories poisoned by artistic emissions. In the long sequence of Peter's encounters in Iraq – such is the substance of the poem included here – he is in danger from warlike Americans and fantasy WMDs, and intent on saving Alfred Ayer, renowned English linguistic philosopher. The further Harry seems from taking horror and extremity seriously, the more the poem insists that while language can never intercept an incoming missile, it can light up a moral scene as nothing else can. Harry is of the school of Carroll, Lear, e.e. cummings and Lawrence Durrell, except that she would deny any identifying label. For me she is the most arresting poet writing in Australia today.

John Kinsella's 'The Vital Waters' is very different. It is a Guide Book sortie around Cambridge, that beautiful but complacent university city in chilly East Anglia. Kinsella works there part of the year: he divides the rest of his time between Ohio and Western Australia. His poem is not a satire, and is remarkably good-natured, but it resembles one of these exposés that television entices us to believe are truthful secret histories. Under the benign, even celebratory tone, as of a man on a bus conducting a load of tourists, a very sharp intelligence is at work. The style is dexterous and audacious, something unusual in a poem of this kind.

Fay Zwicky's 'Makassar, 1956' is different again. With admirable lack of patronage of her younger self, she recounts adventures on her first foray from Australia en route to Europe and High Culture. Many of us have passed this way, but mostly we have ignored the stopping-off points – we were waiting to exclaim over Paris and London. Undeterred by the piled-up quandaries of multiculturalism, Zwicky sticks to her subject in a leach-like way. The first impressions of a youthful perception are treated with complete honesty. This is poetry alerted by its own serendipity.

Editors like to take biopsies of the body politic of poetry. What are the subjects which move poets today? Has formality been wholly overthrown by experiment and improvisation? Where are the Women Poets? This group is certainly here in decently representative number. The Older Masters put in some laps of honour – Bruce Beaver, Bruce Dawe, Keith Harrison, Clive James, Evan Jones and Chris Wallace-Crabbe. Before we salute those who may be considered (at least by elderly editors) newcomers, let us celebrate the many who are in their flourishing early maturity – Peter Goldsworthy, who has never let schematic wit drive lyricism from his work; Geoffrey Lehmann, a composer of reality's daisy-chains; Jennifer Maiden, whose verse develops in ever-widening circles round the topic which made her famous, 'The Problem of Evil'; John Tranter, consummate experimenter, always in close communication with the core body of poetry in Europe and the United States; and Les Murray, our Captain, never frightened of being put into an open boat by his mutinous crew.

Then there are MTC Cronin, who lights up language at a touch; Michael Farrell and Chris Edwards, two agents of a dispersing avant-garde; Philip Hammial, who is developing a new line in out-of-the-way pilgrimage; Dorothy Porter, sister to the immortal Stevie Smith; Peter Rose, urban moralist and latter-day Hazlitt; and Craig Sherborne, the most promising shuffler of the cards in our current pack of authentic monsters.

As an overseas editor, I feel I am under some obligation to discuss the state of poetry in Australia. I think I should respond to this with an unevasive answer: it is in as healthy a condition as anywhere else. At least, this applies to the stuff itself and the attitudes of those who write it. However, if I look at the market for poetry in Australia, I am considerably less sanguine. Australian publishers who have Poetry Lists are dwindling. Magazines, other than the specialist journals devoted principally to promoting poetry, are hardly committed. University departments prefer to concentrate on arts they think more relevant – biography, fiction, literary theory, cinema, and politics. The bookshops are pretty dire. The boom in verse I noticed in the seventies when I first returned to Australia has disappeared. Poetry is being taught widely as practice and as criticism, but more usually in semi-official schools. The most likely question put to any famous litterateur at a festival will be – 'How much money do you make?' or 'How do I get my novel published?' It seems that poetry is doomed to never become a spectator sport, but always a practitioner's.

Within these covers are recorded the names of the good angels who are helping poetry in Australia – *Heat*, *ABR*, *Famous Reporter*, *Salt*, *Blue Dog*, *The Age*, *The Australian*, *Island*, *Quadrant*, and the rest. Such papers and magazines deserve the most honourable of mentions. Meanwhile, I, as editor and compiler, invite you to investigate a harvest of the best poetry Australia was happy to publish in the previous twelve months.

BRUCE BEAVER

A SCHIZOID POEM

Too much of what I have to say now is ridiculous –
Not enough of what I have to say now is ridiculous.
For I am cursed or blessed with a schizoid mind
that sees things alternately tragically and comically.
It affects all the major issues in my life.
If a friend or a loved one dies I see it as a tragic deprivation
or a comical mistake in which they finally freed themselves
     of me.
The pathetic fallacy of a thunderstorm suddenly becomes
     a giant joke
in bad taste, of course. Too often they rattle my filled teeth
     only.
When I was much, much younger it all interfered with my
     sexual ventures.
A mole on a bare back became a melanoma
certain sounds became irresistibly funny.
Alas now that I'm old this Janus mind still bullies my
     decisions.
If I have to choose between marmalade and honey
in one cast of mind the oranges will be little sun-gods
disintegrated and though delectable brutally sacrificed
in another they will be laughably acquiescent to the toast.
Or the honey seems an unforgivable rape of many hives

on one hand, and on the other the comical thigh scouring
of many single minded and basically sexless insects.

_____

Southerly

JUDITH BEVERIDGE

THE SHARK

We heard the creaking clutch of the crank
as they drew it up by cable and wheel
and hung it sleek as a hull from the roof.

Grennan jammed open the great jaws
and we saw how the upper jaw hung from
the skull. We flinched at the stench of blood

that dripped on the fishhouse floor, and
even Davey – when Grennan reached in
past the scowl and the steel prop for the

stump – just about passed out. The limb's
skin had already blanched, a sight none
of us could stomach, and we retched –

though Grennan, cool, began cutting off
the flesh in knots, slashing off the flesh
in strips; and then Davey flensing and

flanching – opened up the stomach and
the steaming bowels . . . gulls circled like
ghouls. Still they taunt us with their cries

and our hearts still burn inside us when
we remember, how Grennan, with a tool
took out what was left of the child.

Heat

JAVANT BIARUJIA

ICARUS

I can understand how mentally deranged or overdosed people plunge to their deaths from high places, in the belief they could fly. At the fort above Grenoble, I peered over the precipice and imagined how wonderful it would feel to leap into pure space and be carried away by a thermal updraught over the terracotta roofs of the city and beyond, to the snow-capped mountains, past Chambéry, with Hannibal's elephant fountain, past Megève, where George Segal and Glenda Jackson crashed their cars into each other, in *Lost and Found*, and even as far as Mont Blanc itself!

Human birds must have lived here for, on the very crest of Mont Saint-Eynard, there are remnants of another, older fort. Almost a kilometre and a half up in the sky. Who were these people's foe? Did they believe they were incarnations of eagles? To reach the fort, I must take a *téléphérique*, a kind of chair-lift, with the chairs encased inside a Perspex bubble. As I ascended over the Isère, and the older part of town, it occurred to me how much my life has been like living in a bubble. I am rootless; I am ignorant of the state of affairs in the world; I understand so little of the workings of the places I visit, always the stranger in town. I have basic wants: a roof over my head for the night, something to eat, a good bottle of wine on occasion, some human warmth every now and then.

A bubble is a *paradis artificiel*, then? A temporary state, selfish, not bound by responsibilities. One in which I am free to roam without a care in the world. It is also a fragile state, suspension . . . if the cable were to break . . . ?

Heat

MTC CRONIN

THE DUST IN EVERYTHING

Remember the dust in everything?
Star-creature, heart-creature, person-creature.
There is no guarantee that there will be any hours after your
   death.
You might share your death with the world.
Like a poison or a flower and the knowledge of when they are
   one.
The mauve gums in your mouth will fade and then darken.
'Still to do' will take on its crown and its ruin.
The rice you did not eat will not be eaten.
Left on your plate it haunts the starving person you have
   become.
Your bag is dropped by the door.
In a short time from now it will be shaken and hung.
Never was there an emptier bag.
Packed full with the belongings of one dead.
They are like dust.
What fitted in your hand, dust.
What followed the shape of your shoulders, dust.
What you unfolded and read and wept for, dust.
Dust, the moon; dust, the rhododendron.
Dust the look from another's eyes.
And you have an empty head.

Into it has flown the whole first night after your death.
All those stars and their habit of reminder.
Using light to keep themselves alive beyond the grave.
You think with them and remember the dust in everything.
Star-creature, heart-creature, person-creature.
With what patience and no want you now become.
Anything you might once have wanted to divine.
The brick of a house, a juice-bead.
Reality berries, god's lost bleat in an ear.
The persistent energy of your own thoughts.
There is no guarantee that there will be any hours before your
     death.
All might disappear, like a journey.
The dust might leave in the mind of a genius.
And the dead might never have lived.
Not born, not unborn, renouncing renunciation.
The rice they ate was never eaten.
The rice is dust.
No, dust's ramification.
Like a little speck it floats.
You learnt to dance that way and to do everything.

_____

Meanjin

Bruce Dawe

OTHERNESSES OTHER THAN OUR OWN

Sometimes I think it is in other natures that we understand
our own dominating inconsequence in the world: the cattle,
sheep, horses in a paddock, what are they doing there? who
bid them proliferate? So often I have wanted to ask them all:
who sent you? what do you make of your presence here?
do you ever have a sense of its fleetingness under this ironic
and brooding sky, slumped together under the trees' benison,
        or heads
to the wind, bearing the incomprehensible
burden of weather, of mysterious night, of man's neglect or
brutally calculating interest? The mother-love of ewes
for their lambs, of mares for their foals, the treeless plain,
the swallows' swoop, the hawks' glide, galahs rising in noisy
crowds like soccer hooligans over the saltbush, or from
specially appointed eucalypts, weebills interposing
their tentative questioning, the pathos of all creatures and
not least ourselves, troubles me like the shadow of the wind
breathing its knowledgeable acrostics to the clouds.

Southerly

BRETT DIONYSIUS

---

from THE EXTINCTION SONNETS

1. GIANT GALAPAGOS TORTOISE

He who put his hands around my plate-size
Self is extinct now. Dry short lives you lot.
Sapas Humana your dream-sea's in drought.
My soft egg yesterdays my beak-shears snip.
Not like your nail-scissors type, selected out
By international flight, your box-cutter RIP.
Days I crossed. Galapagos, Cold English,
Terra nullius, witnessed your species self-
Mutilation twice. As you died, I only grew.
Survived your fashions, your skin theories.
My advice: carry your own home with you.
Outgrew his shell-size I think, Mr Darwin.
Now I'm with Steve Irwin at Australia Zoo.
I *Harriet*, time-lord tortoise: outlive him too.

2. PARADISE PARROT

It was a scud that killed us: a Rockhampton Rocket
Or such. You don't believe me? Officially they'll put
It down to loss of understorey, clear felled Brigalow

Forest for cloven terrorists / plant helots that obeyed.
But who knows what happened better than the dead?
It was your Sunday tennis that did it. Your habit
For social interaction, district gossip, loam slide rules.
You didn't think, but then we didn't either. Stupid really
With all these trees around to build in termite mounds.
If only your species had selected grass or clay earlier.
Or played another sport? Indoor cricket? Darts?
We know one thing for sure. Don't come to us
For advice on nest protection. We'll drop a game
Or worse, choke: a species double fault.

Meanjin

ALISON EASTLEY

PIPE DREAMS

I misheard lyrics playing on the stereo
when I was waiting for mascara to dry.
It emphasised the luminous shine of
wanting you because all afternoon
I'd fantasised about what we could do
with soft leather. If this is less controlled
than craving a Moroccan market place
where women wear black and men
escape to pray every Friday, I'd say
desire could be the tantalising lower lip
on the mouth of the Mediterranean Sea.

Salt-lick: New Poetry

STEPHEN EDGAR

PICTURES OF LOVE

1

At one slight tug the loosened belt
Undoes its bow and now the slack
And lapsing folds of fabric melt
Across her shoulderblades and back,

Over her buttocks, down her thighs,
Like lotion, lucent, smooth and cool,
Until about her feet it lies
In a still rippling gathered pool,

From which she steps to his embrace –
That naked garment to redress
Her nakedness – where face to face
They form two parts of one caress.

As when in scientific probes
The brain is wired and stimuli
Reveal its efflorescent lobes
To burst in colours, flare and die,

So where their bodies touch, the pressure
Of limb on limb, the lingering stroke
Of fingertips, the inward pleasure
Held beyond breathing, all provoke

Pictures that flourish in the mind,
So intimate and so intense
That to each other they seem blind.
They watch them with another sense

While through the images they gasp
Towards each other where they lie
Locked in an ever tighter clasp,
Lest they themselves should flare and die.

2

The casual inspector
Might look on them as frauds,
A cold waxwork attraction
Shown at Madame Tussaud's.
A word from the director,
Though, summons them to action.

Under the lights' enormous
And vitalising charge,
The camera-worked emotions
In which they loom so large,
Our two aroused performers
Rise to their moist devotions.

Limbs separate and tangle,
Open and close: how much
The lens's lurid hocus
Brings near enough to touch.
There's no forbidden angle,
No unimagined focus.

And should we glimpse their faces
Like any other part,
The view's hardly invasive
Of either mind or heart;
The pleasure-blind grimaces
They play are unpersuasive,

But simply moves obeying
A script, the formula
Their tireless bodies follow
Like two automata
Incessantly portraying
Senses of which they're hollow.

Those eyes grant no disclosure
Of any scene within,
Only an illustrated
Extension of the skin,
A quite selfless exposure
That says less than is stated.

Our revels now are ended.
They fall back side by side –
Like Frankenstein's numb creature
Laid out by his numb bride
Before the charge intended
To quicken limb and feature.

3

The doors are locked, the curtains drawn.
Loosed by enclosure they begin
Dismantling the long discipline
That holds them between dawn and dawn.

The sheets that mantle the embowment
Made by their bodies crease and move
About them as they strive to prove
Time prisoner to one slow moment.

And as in the advertisement
A woman wading through the cool,
Thigh-pleated waters of a pool
Tugs at it with an indolent

And trailing hand and peels away
The surface like a silken shawl,
So in their coupling as they sprawl
And ruck the bedclothes in their play,

More than the bedclothes are pulled free.
The carpets are dragged up and wound
About them, the four walls around
The bed surrender pliantly

In rumpled folds, the windows dyed
With green leaf-netted light collapse
And join the fabric which enwraps
Their blind arrival. But outside

A bus brakes. In the market, crowds
Are haggling. Little boys compete
While sparrows peck the windy street.
The sky makes history in the clouds.

Island

CHRIS EDWARDS

VERILY

In *Capital!* and in his earlier writings
they said he was living in a room by himself,
a Joseph Cornell album
owed to and demanded by
the principle of identity
not two minutes ago. Lo
and Behold were coeval developments:
long before *ad infinitum*, dependable
clockwork etc., the problem was the idea
of deciding. Wherever
he went he saw semi-
quavers – gold, then salt, then
today sand and stones – meaning
'to reveal oneself'
piecemeal, e.g. 'problematic
Handbuch enclosure' –
oak or willow, hard to say which –
whilst shepherding the huluppu-tree
via Tablet XII, plus notes.
Yet there were dates
to be determined,
crates to be unpacked:
he'd tracked them down

through nether regions
hatched from the *holus bolus*.
Servant or priest of 40 or of $^2/_3$,
he was doomed to live exhausted,
out of breath,
not words.

_____

Boxkite

DIANE FAHEY

FALL

Ivy infests more shrubs, the more I clear;
each winter drop seeds a new sucker.
Ambushed, I meet hard earth, my ankles
a momentary sideways hinge: a fall
too swift to remember. Each foot now wears
a sock of yellow-blue-green – the mottled
map laid bare by a peeling fresco.

Day after day I lie curled inside time,
the mind-shadows cast by so much death
in strange abeyance. There's a rest from
onwardness, too: my body saturated with
its life so far, sealed against dissolution.
My feet are growing wings from the bruises,
storing strength for the next reach of the journey.

Blue Dog: Australian Poetry

MICHAEL FARRELL

POEM WITHOUT DICE

there are only two types of movies worth watching
movies taken of a road & movies taken from a road
this assertions of course open to criticism & possibly outright
attack just think how political discourse is altered when you
exchange all the vs for ws or js for ks for that matter
the poem taxis & avoids the spot on the lesion of ac
or aesthetic correctness preferring a kind of continental
sprawl the long line favoured by for example frank ohara
suitable for the beach or sydneys or melbournes streets
its no surprise to be a little heavier around the waist
& if you can get home without donating too much loose
      change
& other sentimental objects to the world hey thats
doing well besides my bloods internationally worthless
anyone can carry on in this way to the readers anxiety
inside time & expectations of nourishment if not
from the page then a passing waiter is your bladder
in order an ultimately meaningless question designed
by waiters to annoy & discourage diners from requesting
too many glasses of water meaninglessness accrues
like anything & any sense of the reader becomes faint
imagine stevie smith on her death bed playing an atheist
bishop she calls for her cat & draws him a door there

rudolph like many cats named after reindeer theres where im
going through the monsignor door like so many santas to
   follow

Eureka Street

PETER GOLDSWORTHY

AUSTRALIA

Our earthen dish is seven parts water,
one part china, and a tiny bit japanned.
Its spread of foods is well-presented:
ice sculptures at both poles, and licking-salt
elsewhere. Give me a lever large enough –
a cosmic fork or skewer – and I would take it
to a table: its sherbet fizz of surf,
the creamy ice-cones of its toothy alps,
the spice of islands dotted here and there
like cloves jammed in an onion. Turning
this common dish as slowly as a day, I'd taste
the sweet-and-sour river deltas, the swamps
about its world wide waist, all of which
smell fishy. As do many maps of Tasmania,
most of them in other places: forest fuzz
itchy with green pubic life. Lastly comes
our smaller plate, single and tectonic:
our turf, or lack of it, our baked and gritty
crust, lightly watered, sifter dusted,
and sarcastic with odd hints of eucalypt.
Its thousand mile creek tastes too salty,

its muddy waters barely moving, but still
moving enough to stir a homesick heart.

Quadrant

PHILIP HAMMIAL

PORRIDGE

It's that kind of day as we cross a frontier
into Turkey, two hitchhikers in a car
with smugglers from Istanbul. All manner of vehicles
on this road into the city – a horse-drawn hearse followed
by a three-wheeled Messerschmitt with two flat tires
followed by seven nuns on bicycles built for two. The
kind of day when the nuns end up on our hotel, in
the room next door, but luckily
they've brought their own porridge
so we won't have to give them any of ours
& as for the proliferation of skin in this poem
that we're concocting under some duress
(don't say you haven't noticed) they leave it up to us
to do with it what we will: tune in
to the Whiskey Show where every launched ship
is hulled with it, the Bosporus as busy as a kitchen
in the Topkapi Palace where funerals around the clock
are the norm. But not to worry: the minarets
up on the Stamboul skyline won't start spouting smoke
just because our neighbours are out on their balcony
giving the locals an eyeful. It's not Auschwitz. It's
Istanbul, & in any case we've changed hotels, too
much noise from those silly girls shouting their prayers

all night like rappers at a Harlem rent party & we
weren't invited, probably because of our association
with those smugglers who brought us here,
their parting gift of porridge worth its weight in gold.

Blue Dog: Australian Poetry

JENNIFER HARRISON

THE LOVELY UTTERLY COLD SNOW
Melbourne Writers' Festival 2003

the writers sit behind
water-jugs, corncob-miked

their talk, ghost ribbons
touching our throats

Kandahar, Laos, Hutu
the names graceful, and theoretical

each session
has the empty chair
of an absent author

the gesture
strangely bouyant

a piety
to remind
this noisy church of words
of the elsewhere voices

in grotesque vignette
in butchered villages, verandahs breathe:

that dress, that land
that skirt

that milk
leaking from a swollen bowl
its clay cracked by a sword

is memory then the soul

and grief a claustrophobic space
where nothing tastes
of grammar's lovely utterly cold snow?

here, the author's signature
is absurdly sought

as though the empty page
requires its spoor of fame

our applause folding back
upon the hand and its bones

Salt-lick: New Poetry

KEITH HARRISON

AN OLD WOMAN SINGS IN HER BED BUT MAKES NO SOUND

The summer night is dangerous and deep.
I lie, dead still, aware of the tiniest sounds
Being so full of joy I cannot sleep.

The night is dangerous, so many lives.
I love my husband well. A sharp moon
Rubs the spine of the barn. Nothing moves.

So many lives for the small years that remain.
My skin more wrinkled than a withered prune,
I study my hand and no word can explain.

You are a kindly man who's fast decaying.
Why am I so content tonight to watch my hands
Now that the rooster wakes while I'm betraying

All that we built, and everything winds down.
I study my hands, dissolving into nothing:
The wind-washed cocklebur in which we'll drown.

Why am I so content? Will we rise again
As dragonflies, perhaps, or gleaming birds?
Who knows? Only one thing is plain.

Now that the rooster crows – not once, but three
Times three times thirty-three I am betraying
All that we built, betraying shamelessly

Because of a plume of pick-up dust that carries
Him here, no god but a pillar of solid flame
Smelling of roadside tar and a crush of berries

To stretch me out and crack and almost crack,
Again and again, and maybe again today
With a plume of dust winding along the track.

I love my husband well, nothing will change.
So many lives to live: I have no shame.
I love you well, and everything is strange.

The summer night is dangerous and deep
But, being completely taken by that flame,
I am so full of joy I cannot sleep.

Australian Book Review

J.S. HARRY

JOURNEYS WEST OF 'WAR'
from *Peter Henry Lepus in 'Iraq'*

1

Where is he? Peter Henry Lepus wonders.
He is squatting – well past sunset –
in one of the few
mapped
    depressions
in Iraq's Western Desert,
ears turned to one side,
listening to the 'Wind on Fencing Wire.'
Its whistly noises seem to come from somewhere near.
He's heard this CD played before
when he was chewing creek-side grass that grew
– hard, tough, & slightly sour –
near a roadworkers' camp at Oodnadatta.
He remembers a composer from Western Australia
who worked with 'natural sounds,'
& a tape recorder.

Coming through strange cracklings
& noises of static
like those emitted
by Josh Smith's

radio
in Baghdad,
he hears an alien voice
speculate:
Maybe it's the wind
that played on the Rabbit-Proof Fence
in 'Australia . . . del Espiritu Santo'?

Who is listening?
Is it Professor Ayer, he thinks, or *could it*
be Joshua Smith?

He'd left Joshua Smith
walking the Baghdad streets, dodging car bombs,
looking for his wives,
& travelled, mostly at night,
                    eventually hitching a ride
with a scrawny desert-bound camel
                    – 'strayed' – it'd said,
from one of the city's bazaars, where,
being long unsold, it had suspected,
its merchant was going to kill it.
Too skinny to fetch a good price I am,
it'd snorted noisily, then had harrumphed.
Thin camels get eaten in Baghdad.
Peter had not enjoyed the ride.
Its back is not easy to sit on, he'd concluded.

Had been glad to leap off when the camel bent legs
& collapsed to rest on the riverbed at sunset.

Peter's looking for Professor Alfred Jules Ayer,
& a group of British
phenomenalist philosophers, who wish
to discuss
the professor's work,
                    & to experience
the desert's mirages.
Ayer is observing the behaviour
of wind, sun, & sand.
When Peter last saw him
Professor Ayer was on a camel heading east,
the pursuing philosophers
far behind him.
They seemed to march as a group, their faces
red, their knees, red, too.
A few, Peter saw, had blisters,
sun-dried, gummed with sand.
Some legs looked very white
where the socks had fallen down.
Peter's camel 'd not been impressed,
nor wanted to go any closer.
It'd harrumphed again, which Peter
had learnt, by this time, was a sign of
displeasure. He'd been disappointed.
He wants to gain answers to his questions

about the roles
the words
    'language'
        'truth'
            & 'logic'
have played
in Professor Ayer's life.

Peter's found an abandoned philosophy notebook,
with some writings about 'Illusion.'
                  Working his way round boulders
& up the bank, cautiously he stops,
ears lowered & flattened,
to observe, keeping as close as possible to the ground.
There is someone sitting, knees crossed,
with a camera round his neck. The 'Wind on Fencing Wire''s
being twanged across the desert
from a radio beside a bed roll & a pack.
This person is talking
perhaps to himself or into a little machine
with an aerial, positioned on a plastic sack,
beside a baby-carrots' can, which Peter, inching
towards, sees is empty.

The man, Max Strang, is testing a mobile phone,
which he's just acquired, he says,
from one of the 'post-Saddam entrepreneurs.'

34

Yeah, there've been more bombs, one near the airport,
there's trouble getting round, street sniping
still going on – some Yanks got shot.
The voice sounds like one Peter's heard before
on Sydney radio, talking from Iraq.
It's in mid-flow . . .
He's had no real scoops to send, before, or after, the war,
failed to get himself embedded, with the Coalition Forces
or with the Yanks; the local TV
won't use him, his Arabic's not good –
besides, it's the wrong kind,
not Formal, literate, written . . .
but street speech
he's picked up outside Iraq. He's come to the desert
to tape the nocturnal hyenas.
Thinks he might sell
some Iraqi 'natural sound'
to a friend who's a muso
at Griffith, just moved from Woy Woy,
near where
Spike Milligan used to live. If that doesn't work,
he's heard a rumour about some gold . . .
& a man who's lost a lot of wives . . .

He is talking to someone called 'Weasel' Smith,
who writes under the pseudonym 'Botany' Jones.

                                                            Peter,
who has uncomfortable memories

associated with the English rural weasel,
begins to twitch,
anticipating mention of
their custom of 'eating rabbit.' He watches
Max Strang's mouth & throat, trying
to forget weasels,
& their larger cousins, the stoats,
&, to remember,
he, Peter Henry Lepus, squats,
as a scribe,
in a different country,
having travelled
into another time, as well as text.

He thinks of his *Rabbit History of Philosophers*,
of where to begin it,
whether with Zarathustra, in Persia,
(six twenty-eight to five thirty-one B.C.) or with
the one called Thales, who's said
to have travelled to 'Babylon,' which,
Peter's read, lies south of Baghdad,
& of what the Flowerbed Rabbit would say . . .
Wherever she is, he cannot reach her from here.
Dejectedly, he begins to listen to Max Strang
angrily informing Weasel Smith

about his failed feature story – on how
half a million Iraqi children under five

are estimated to have died
between nineteen hundred & ninety,
when the UN trade sanctions were imposed
& nineteen hundred & ninety-eight,

as a result of poor health of mothers,
the more general
collapse of health services,
& the lack of power
for the country's water supply
– an ongoing problem – . He castigates editors.
Weasel Smith cuts in, very loudly, *one dead Aussie now – with a*
good shot – taken alive & smiling, in Iraq –
that might make the news.

Max Strang begins to run his fingers
through his greasy hair & talk about
how long it is since he's been under a shower.
He's decided.
He doesn't want to make the news any more.

Over his shoulder, clinging to the strap of his camera,
Peter sees a tiny form emerge.
It has eight thin legs & looks like a baby Huntsman Spider.
I'm Clifta Webb, it says.
Do you know the way to Persia?
It is wearing tiny red cargo pants, over its four
lower legs, the 'waist' ending only part way up

a small, distended, glistening abdomen.
You could go down the Shatt-al-Arab,
Peter says, thinking fast.
Why do you want to go to Persia?

Though, on the map, Iraq & Iran nestle together,
he does not think so tiny a creature as this junior spider
could travel, by land, so far, directly east,
walking on those short eight legs –
perhaps even through the dangers of Central Baghdad . . .

Perhaps you could drop yourself onto a boat;
you would need to travel down the Tigris
or the Euphrates, to get to the Shatt-al-Arab,
then perhaps . . . do some floating . . . to reach Iran –
maybe jump onto one of the minesweepers . . .

His nose & forehead wrinkle.
She would have to get to a river with water, first.
Clifta is starting to spring about restlessly
on Max Strang's long black oily neck hairs
just above his open collar. Max is now talking to Weasel Smith's
girlfriend, calling her
darling, very softly, over & over.
He does not seem to notice Clifta.
I've seen boats with thatched tops –
Iraqis living on them –
on one of the rivers,

Peter begins slowly. He is thinking
such a thatched top
would make a good place
for a spider to hide in.
Clifta stares at Peter. His eyes are big & dark.
He does not look like a Huntsman Spider.
He does not look at all like a great huntsman . . .
She begins to recite:
– *They say the Lion and the Lizard*
keep
The Courts where Jamshyd gloried
and drank deep:
And Bahram, that great Huntsman –
the Wild Ass
Stamps o'er his Head, and he lies fast
asleep.
Peter looks hard at Clifta. He can see her better
now Max Strang has turned his neck.
The light from Max Strang's torch
makes scarlet specks glitter on her cargo pants
as she moves around his hair.
She will have to take those cargo pants off, Peter thinks,
if she is to travel
less noticeably
on the pale
desert sand. He asks
Are 'Jamshyd' & 'Bahram' philosophers?,
&, with less interest, belatedly,

because, after some thought,
he still does not understand:
What does your poem . . . mean?

Clifta does not answer directly.
She heard it from her mother,
while roaming in a Sydney park
around her mother's hairy legs
amid hundreds of other week-old sibling spiders.
She thinks she might be related
to the great Huntsman of the *Rubaiyat*. Since the poem
has been translated from the Persian, she has stowed away,
on the person of the newsman, & in his camera case,
to go to Persia, to try to gather 'facts'
for the Huntsman's Family Tree.

2 *What Is 'The World'?*

What is 'The World'?
Peter has read
in the Hindu Upanishads
that 'the world before creation
was water.' If you could find
'the world before creation,' you could find
where water might have been
perhaps, & perhaps,
there might still be some there, he thinks.

He has been reading about the Pre-
Socratic philosophers – east & west –
from some small books he found in English
in an empty house outside Baghdad,

& wondering, for the umpteenth time,
where his *Rabbit History of Philosophers*
should begin. Perhaps there was a primordial,
even famous, rabbit philosopher
from whom the Pre-Socratics
made their start?
When he talks of this to Clifta, she jumps sideways
& begins excitedly to talk.
She has an in-the-beginning story to tell.
Once was a female Huntsman Spider, from whose egg-sac
sprang earth, water, sky, & 'world,' & from whom
the first lemon-scented gum trees grew, as well
as the angophoras, the acacias,
& the Sydney blue gums that were made
for Huntsman Spiders to live & hunt beneath.

Peter is reminded Clifta travelled to Iraq
under or around the collar of,
or perhaps, in the camera case that hung from,
Max Strang's hairy Sydney neck.
She is not an English spider.

He worries. If she is too small
to make a web, what does she eat?

They are travelling down the riverbed, looking
for the camel, in case it can be persuaded
to take Clifta, not to Baghdad, but to somewhere
lower down, where, on Peter's map, the Euphrates
has water, & there may be boats . . .
It's a city camel. Peter thinks it may not
have realised, initially, the north-western channels
have no water. Eventually, it, too, will need
to drink, it may, even now,
be travelling south & east . . .
Clifta is scuttling along, quite fast
but she seldom
goes in a straight line
down the riverbed, she inspects behind rocks
& large pebbles. Each time, he
has to stop, & wait for her to re-emerge.
He has no idea what she is looking for.

They've left Max Strang waiting for the desert hyenas
which he is hoping
to tape. They have seen no hyenas.
Max Strang was on his mobile again,
speaking softly to Weasel Smith's girlfriend,
trying to persuade her to give up on Weasel Smith
& come & join him, soon, in Iraq.

Peter's learnt Max has a ride
back to Baghdad, arranged with an Iraqi
who has camels, but who will not arrive
for about a week.
Max Strang is a patient man. He has
water & a tin pyramid of cans.

                                    For hyenas he is
prepared to wait.
            Clifta
had been impatient.
She'd wanted
to get off his neck.

It is not happy travelling. The sun moves slowly overhead.
Clifta's begun another recitation of the poem
Arachnid Fitzgerald translated from the Persian,
& although there have been intermissions, when she scuttled
Peter, by now, is becoming pretty bored with it.
He is also itchy, gritty, & more than a little hungry.
A wind has arisen, on the desert above,
which blows more sand into his fur, even though
they are below the worst of it. Faintly he hears
English voices, above the wind,
& struggles
through slipping sand
up the bank. The last two stragglers from the hiking group
of phenomenalist philosophers
have caught the reluctant camel. One is attempting

to drag it by a rope, dodging
its snorts & attempts to bite.
The other, doing nothing, stands well behind.
They are headed back towards Baghdad. Their water cans &
backpacks have been secured to the camel's sides.
Peter can hear the camel harrumphing crossly:
they have not thought to give it any water. Baghdad
is exactly where it does not want to go.
Abruptly it sits down, refusing to move.
What kind of 'Phenomenology'
are they studying, Peter wonders. He has read –
a very little – about Husserl's
'Realist Phenomenology,' & that
Husserl maintained 'the mind'
& nothing else in 'the world'
has 'a directedness' towards something
outside itself. He thinks about the camel
which seems to be directed, now,
towards gaining water, & of Clifta
who seems to be directed backwards in time
towards locating an ancient starting point
of Huntsman Spiders . . .

Peter has no idea how many books
it might take, to do
the Huntsman's Family Tree,
nor to trace Clifta's ancestors back
to the civilisation

of Ancient Persia.
He has seen spiders' webs glistening at night
the lines going out . . . perhaps . . . towards
the stars; he imagines, though her search
could not be infinite, it might seem so . . .
Husserl wrote: there always has to be a
'consciousness
              of something,' & whether,
or not, there is a 'world of objects'
outside the objects of our consciousness,
can, quite simply, be bracketed out.

Clifta, Peter thinks, wants to find
something in 'the world
that is bracketed out.'
              If she
finds 'Persia,'
she can, perhaps,
gain sense-data
about her ancestor,
the Huntsman of the *Rubaiyat*,
& she won't need to prove,
Peter thinks, with effort,
that her 'facts'
'exist'
outside her consciousness . . .

From the channel of the Euphrates, he sees
her tiny indignant form emerge. *I want to go to Persia NOW,*
she says. The English philosophers
have given up,
have unloaded the camel, & abandoned it. They
have taken their desert-sand-coloured selves
in their pale sandals
away, quite fast. The camel staggers up.
There is water in the river
to the south-east, Peter says. *If you take me – &,* he points, to the
agitated tiny spider, *I think I can find*
the main channel of the Euphrates, where we can drink. If we
follow it down to the Delta, there'll be date palms, shelter
& plants to eat . . . He turns to face Clifta.
In the Delta, you will be closer to 'Persia' –
it is called 'Iran' now – &, in the Hawr-al-Hammar,
there may be many boats . . .

Heat

KIRWAN HENRY

BEE SEASON

December covers
My walls with bees

My ankle
And my shin
Are stung
But I like bees
If not for their sting
Then for their stripes

They fit them
Oddly
Like babies
With eyebrows
Too big
For their faces
And I cannot help
But laugh
At their plural addiction
To direction –
Always needing

More than one
Way to go
But never knowing which

Heat

GRAEME HETHERINGTON

ATHENIAN WOLVES

The Greeks in the Zappeion feed
A battered old wolf snarling 'Set
Me free to get my own.' In thread-
Bare, dulling coat, I'm much the same,
But better off, having escaped

In middle age from childhood's cage
Of wounds into self-exile, though,
In vaulted concrete cave with tiles,
It's better housed than I among
Low life. Respecting me as one

Of them, their voices drop, as in
My room, or on long cheerless streets
At night, alone, cold and grey, on legs
Thinning under my bulk, I hunt
My family down in packs of poems.

Quadrant

49

RICHARD HILLMAN

THE BIG WET TAKES HOLD

now we've arrived at the gates of paradise
i expect to read about the running of the horses
through the streets of tumut next spring
how the buses for bong bong picnic races
were diverted for the day

now they've run off those missionaries
from the cultural heartland
we will see a few more egrets
running for president on the edge of lake eyre
calling *toujours les poubelles, toujours les poubelles*

now summer is over, the rates have risen
over garbage collection in the upper house
someone is always walking out
for the annual running of the willing
through the streets of canberra

and now in your eye it's pamplona
all over again, looking forward
to the running of the bulls through
the streets of bathurst at the start
of every football season someone

will wear something just as ridiculous
as those te kuiti sheep on his sleeve
will pretend to mourn the trampled child
in the midst of aberration though
the running of the magpies through

the streets of collingwood will make
good tv, i will still require directions
to arabanoo antique and auction house
for bargain bob is a chocolaty kind of cockatoo
deja vu re-run of australian story

hicks versus . . . the bird of unkindness
is an eagle, i want to see the running
of the eagles through woomera
beside all those ashen grey and black
varieties of wildlife jumping fences

trying to get out of the way when
the abc goes on another rampage
filming missile testing operations
of birds enjoying their english breakfast
with floyd at the back door playing

golf with the cat before stepping inside
to watch the running of the dogs
from the flower box on the window sill
the world looks small and frightening
and crawling with space we can see

the running of the emus into their holes
all over those wide australian sand dunes
everything is olympic flag white running
out of breath keeping the eternal flame alight
at least until the game season ends

Meanjin

CLIVE JAMES

WILLIAM DOBELL'S CYPRIOT

The Cypriot brought his wine-dark eyes with him
Along with his skin and hair. He also brought
That shirt. Swathes of fine fabric clothe a slim
Frame with a grace bespeaking taste and thought.

Australia, 1940. There were few
Men native-born who had that kind of style.
Hence the attention Dobell gave the blue
Collar and cuffs, to make us pause awhile

And see a presence that did not belong.
This sitter, sitting here, caught by this hand?
Caught beautifully. No there is nothing wrong
About this transportation to Queensland

Of ancient subtleties. It's merely odd.
A man whom he had loved and seen asleep
The painter painted naked, a Greek god.
But then he had the sudden wit to keep

The clothes, and thus the heritage in the next
Picture. A window from a men's-wear store,
It doubles as the greatest early text
Of the immigration. What we were before

Looks back through this to what we would become.
We see a sense of nuance head our way
To make the raw rich, complicate the sum
Of qualities, prepare us for today.

Now that the day is ours, the time arrives
To remember destiny began as chance,
And history is as frail as human lives.
A young and foreign smile, love at first glance:

Painter and painted possibly first met
Just because one admired the other's tie.
A year old then, I live now in their debt.
This is the way they live. I too will die.

Australian Book Review

JOHN JENKINS

UNDER THE SHADED BLOSSOM

Wallace Stevens (1879–1955), one of America's finest poets, worked life-long as an insurance executive. He first visited Cuba in 1923. Meyer Lansky (1902–1983) was the Mafia's chief deal-maker and strategist in Havana after 1930. The best and the worst: the poem imagines them meeting in 'the Jewel of the Antilles.'

1

Into Havana's noonday glare, Meyer Lansky slips
from the shadowy front of the *Compañía Hotelera*
La Riviera de Cuba. Jumpy at dislocating knee-symbol crashes
of a passing beggar band. But ol' cool eyes doesn't sweat
so quick – bent brim of a pork-pie hat, and tie so thin it's just
one strand of discreet silk. He's absorbing rays on the
stone steps, abstracted for a while, figuring the numbers.
'When I got to the room and the bellhop flicked back them
big curtains! Boy! I could see almost the whole city.
Like it was in my hand. It was the palm trees that got me first.
Every place you see, there was palm trees. It made me feel like
I was back in Miami in the good old days, with Lucky
and them guys. Everything is *here*' – taps brim
again for luck and turns the felt down. *All in my head.*
(Don't never take notes, don't write nothing down.)
'No one comes breathing down your shoulder here.
Which is what I liked feeling. And only ninety miles
from the coast. *Practically America, it is.*' A quick flick

of his tongue, and Lansky skips out into space opening
up around him, the swinging door of a cream Chevrolet,
as the air closes around any trace of the *gringo financier* . . .
some watching window – *Yeh, it only takes one creep.*
Tonight, he'll hit the Hotel Sevilla Biltmore, the Gran,
the Summer, Chateau Madrid, the dazzling Sans Souci,
La Concha, spin the wheels, catch the acts, and collect up big.
Has just signed the Cuban American Realty Company.
Even sounds legit. 'When me and Lucky first talked about
buying
into real estate, them wise guys thought that we was nuts.
Them guys couldn't see beyond their bowls of spaghetti!'

2

A canary in a cage might seem less free in the morning, though
it sweeten a balcony with song. Mr Stevens looked up
to it, and the white tuft of hair above the broad forehead
also tilted, and a tie was loosed slightly from its pin.
Mr Stevens – Vice President of a prudential company –
today thought the air almost as elemental as the sea,
invisible colours no less vibrant than sun-drenched ones.
Here, time might reveal a succession of facades, each imagined
from pink stone, born of light, atmosphere and sea gloss. It was
close and brisk (he meant the Malecón), where he strolled
and held
upright his sun umbrella and thoughtful face, which held its own
deep quietness, and every shade of light and shade of song.
Mr Stevens,

elaborating a palette both abstract and precise, recalled at
    once the rail
journey down Florida. How Havana always welcomed his
appraisal, how real things revealed themselves to him,
they changed to music, passing an old casino in the park,
    where the bills
of swans had lowered slowly, and lay flat upon the ground beside
their lakes, as he had neared. *For him*? In this way, life gave
its assurance to always change. That something new and
    shining
would appear, or age could shine, or ages again shine – rising
    new from
their patina (*husks, wherein time was cradled*). The stone (he
    noted now)
became rose, and clouds like lightest rose at evening. And
    here, too,
a single quiet dwelt, within the poems he made of things. Or
    orchestras
once played, balloons lifted into tropical night at festivals he
    meant
also to attend. (He was a life lover, after all.) The Malecón
    stirred with
extrinsic music, as did the sea. He watched it lift, through its
    filigreed
notation, leaning into the sea wind with a pencil, and wrote
    now for
an hour, the brine wind turning him neat and leather-bound.

Good, Mr Stevens. Stare out the cannon placements on the
     distant
Moro. They once stared down pirates, protected treasure galleons
in Havana Bay. Here Columbus, that thief of blood and gold,
found a sea road back to Spain. He founded empires.

3

Mr Stevens, as he did every morning, awoke at six
then read for two hours, in his balcony room, becoming
furious at the English *New Statesman*, brought with him
from Hartford, its pungent anti-Americanism, with which
he only part agreed, then the latest on Garbo, his favourite
star. (He dreamed a meeting with her.) Put down the rag,
to re-read then the 'wond'rous play,' as always, ritualistically,
on all his first mornings in Havana. The coffee by his elbow
drifted a delicious lick of steam into old tracery
of leaves wrought in iron, above the wakening street.
His breakfast pleased him: a sweet bean confection, *yep
it was*, with milk curd. *Memo: Ship a packet back to Hartford.*
Especially, he enjoyed the sky, the moist climate of
red flowers and tropical sensuality. And the air. Brine-
scented, special isle. Something soft and sweet about the
air alright, all the way down Florida, peachy cream on skin,
free champagne, and your senses 'inside-out': all around
you, in bright lights, and waiting to be let back in. *Ha! A neat
conceit, brother!* He read on: *Methought the billows spoke
and told me of it . . . The wind did sing it to me . . .*

4

Meyer drank in silence, pernod, for the *woims*, in the early
    morning
hours, with the window of his room open. The Hotel Sevilla
    Biltmore
was built at a cost of 2.5 million pesos, in American gold,
but Meyer, who'd fixed it all up – *nine casinos and six hotels*
    now –
preferred the Hotel Nacional, just like Big Lucky. The old-
style charm and luxury, tempered by good taste. Convenient too
for meets – a salon for Batista's stooges, and private elevator
with gilded ironwork for the tame President himself. Meyer was
pensive, dressed in his underwear. He liked to bathe at
    sunrise, move
at random 'bout the room in the first cool air, sprinkle on talcum
powder, before sitting on that little balcony. It was either pernod
or milk, nothing else. An occasional dame from one of Marina's
houses. But he liked to keep his pecker clean. His wife back
    in the
States: Two daughters. And no nose powder. He liked to keep
    his wig
straight, too. All that crap was for suckers. Funny, how you
    can have
everything, yet the thing that delighted him most was the
    noise
of the waves at night. The pernod looked faintly blue, in this
    light.
Maybe he was getting soft. Later, he would have his driver stop

the car near the old monument to the *USS Maine*, and walk
around a bit, and think. Mostly, he just liked to think. The
　　four New
York families wanted in, but he and Lucky keeps them
　　schmucks
out. An austere life. You go unnoticed. *Don't make waves,*
　　just make bucks. An' you make sure everyone in your
　　operation
behaves. It was just business. *Sure.* Near the monument,
he could walk and think. Away from all the noise and glitz,
the overheated deals and the little wooden balls in the rigged
roulette wheels, in the biggest cat house in the Caribbean.
Breathe sea air without saying a word to no-one. All that fresh
salt air. Or the scenery near *Quinta Avenida* (Fifth Avenue),
was pretty. *A surprise visit maybe . . . that barber shop, where*
the New York capos *hang out Sundays. Short back and insides,*
all round! Schmucks is right! But think it all out first, maybe . . .

5

A big blue bow seemed drawn down to join, *sans* any
seeming, a more cobalt sea, where the earth curved away
under blueflake sky, as Mr Stevens discretely departed
Marina's. *The music crept by me upon the waters*
with its sweet air, thence I have followed it. Still,
picturing somehow an indolent progression of swans,
strolled then past a toothless grandmother with a
basketful of pears for sale. Sadly, an old wall had
absorbed the heat of the sun, and limp leaves fell.

He reached up to a flower – *to touch again the hottest bloom* might become, what? – and chuckled. When writing, he liked to travel alone. Packages of various gourmet foods were already mailed home. Even from here, he could turn the keys to Florida, unlock with cash cosmopolitan yearnings. He was tall, austere, very dignified, an unusual looking man. This day he wore a wide-brimmed Panama, having shed his pinstripes for a light, white suit of cotton. And he loved to walk. He'd just walk round by himself, anywhere. A very slow stride, so as not to miss a thing, and peered deliberately from beneath his brim, peered at everything, intently. There were shops, there were streets, old lanes and ancient shade trees. There was always this and that. There were antique Spanish lamps to collect for a polished table back in Hartford, Connecticut. They revolved, lamp and table, in his mind. He knew the shop was somewhere by, close to his embassy, near the old monument to the *USS Maine* – *Remember the Maine!* had inflamed gimcrack populists and tub thumping senators, jingoistic freebooters with their eyes on the biggest fruit dish in the *Antilles* – Mr Stevens reflected as he turned passed the statue, an odd-looking little guy who shoved past neatly, without looking up. Muttering. Pork-pie hat, face like a cod – dead cold eyes – or maybe more reptilian. Black Italian suit and, to his ear, New York corners in the voice – touch of Jewish, Polish, maybe *Sicilian*? Did he really hear . . . '*I'll fix the schmuck*'?

6

Lunch was not in the least a complete fiasco. The genius
(the spirit) of this island must be a chef. The dishes
so exuberantly, so flawlessly, capturing a mind at play,
in the cuisine sense. And absurd and darting, too, into
lists of ingredients that were displayed on a white
card menu, in elegant gold copperplate. A stellar
bill of fare: Black beans, rice *à la marinera*, Creole
salads, avocado, pineapple and juicy cuts of roast
pork. Crab and *queenconch enchilados*, from the southern
archipelago. Roast breast of flamingo, tortoise stew,
roast tortoise with lemon and garlic, crayfish from
Cojímar, oysters from Sagua and grilled swordfish.
Venison chops from Camagüey, the succulent mystery of
the manatee. Quiet corner, old oak table, amidst the napery
and silver setting. He ate alone. He was alone. He chose
small portions of several dishes, without haste or greed.
He savoured a tropic inventiveness, that took delight
in peculiar combinations. And sent a message with the waiter,
back to the chef: A tip for white hats. *Well done amigo!*
A poet can be gourmet, and executive. Worlds widen
to allow, like a girth let out on holiday, that living should
be lived, enjoyed, an adventure. Here's nice logic for
the prim: poet, rich man, gourmet – appetites are part of
        nature
and, as part of nature, part of us. The waiter then brought
        over
a message on a tray. From the smiling cod man at the bar. Pork-

pie hat. Mr Stevens saw – *him (?)*, *again* – tap his brim when he
looked up. Invitation to share a drink. Odd. There was
      something –
more than – peremptory about it. A message from a *boss*.
Threw the card back on the tray, and made his way across.

7

Lansky met him at the big doorway of the grand casino
of the Hotel Nacional's dining room. The two men
shook hands, and the taller was ushered to the bar,
just in sight of the green-felt tables where louche cards
skimmed and fell. 'Mr Stevens, Meyer Lansky. How
was your meal, Pal?' 'Excellent. How do you know
my name? Are you the manager?' 'Let's say I have an
interest. We like our friends to have a good time here –
to make them feel secure. I take care of people in
Havana.' 'I see.' 'Yeh, Pal. Especially with the quality,
business people from the States. The meal's on me!
Now, let me buy you a drink – and some chips. Black-
jack or craps?' 'Thank you, but I can't accept. I don't gamble.'
'Sure, Pal. Forget the craps. Maybe later. Let's have a drink
and talk. What's your poison? Aged rum, Hatuey beer,
Montecristo cigar? Myself, I drink milk, or pernod – pernod
for the *woims*.' Lansky patted his waist . . . 'You can't be
too careful.' *The guy's a chump*, thought Lansky. *Coulda
turned free chips into notes – just one spin of the wheel.
And if he blew 'em, no loss. Then cut out.* Mr Stevens
sipped his seven-year-old rum. It was honey and fire, burnt

honey and smoke. *Touch of heaven, touch of hell here –*
and fortunes rising, sinking on a whirl. This Mr Lansky
is spruiking for that sweet, ruinous addiction. 'Tell
me, Mr Stevens, what's your game? You do back in the
    States?'
'I'm in insurance. Vice President of the Hartford
Accident and Indemnity Insurance Company. Formerly
of the New York Office of the Equitable Surety Co.
of Saint Louis.' 'Insurance, heh? Well, accidents, Pal –
Well, lotsa people have accidents. Tell you, here I'm
thinking of something big. To roll some big cigars.
Banks, insurance, hotels, airfields – *to bring lotsa stuff*
across – imports, exports. Our peanut people – I mean,
the gold-braid flunkeys – will help the moves. Heard of
the Compañía Hotelera La Riviera de Cuba? Nope.
Well, fine. Here's my card. Maybe we could do a deal.'
'What sort of deal?' Mr Stevens thought, *the world*
suddenly a bauble for agents of a suspect generosity.
What sort of instant business this? It has an odour.
This is some monster of the isle, many legs and hands.
'Tell me, Mr Stevens, can I be straight?' 'Please do so, sir,
you have my word it will go no further. My discretion is
absolute.' *You bet, it is. You bet it won't!* Lansky smiles.
'We're looking for a solid and legit firm for some
tricky mainland deals. What we do and the books
don't need any hard looking at, you understand. Things
sorta go round in slow circles. It ain't so obvious. There's
a code, and lots of just knowing what to do, without

saying much. What you get is paid cash, Pal, a river of cash, to buy up real estate, and lots of gilt policies in case things fall flat. That's the deal. I don't want to say no more for now.'

8

'What say?' *Maybe a photograph next time at Marina's, if the chump says no,* thought Lansky – *Shoulda already done that. Shoulda thought of that, already.* Mr Stevens sighed. *This is a dangerous place. Be careful. He clearly governs this tin heaven. The first act, his gladhand bribe, the next – entrapment. So, the earths alive with creeping men. So, mechanical beetles never quite warm. 'His guilt-edge like poison, given to work a great time after.'* 'Mr Lansky, I thank you for your warm hospitality. And for your interest in our little firm, and your directness. I studied Law at Harvard, and graduated from law school in New York in 1903. I was admitted to the bar a year later. Let me tell you, I have so constituted our company, that all our books are watched by many eyes, and from all sides, all ferociously legal. To have any dealing with me would place your affairs under a scrutiny most intense, almost as a matter of course. But so you don't feel chipped by having your offer returned, let me buy *you* a drink now – a pernod, for the *woims*.' Lansky slapped his new pal on the back. 'Sure Pal, sure. So forget it. Enjoy your stay on old Havana. Tell your friends. As I said, we just like everyone to have a good time. No hard feelings. Sure! In fact, I made the whole pot up. I aint got no companies. I wuz only

raising you, to see your hand. I don't want no crooks
or takers hanging round my casino. Not with all this
moolah in the air. Hey, you did right. You got a flush there,
Pal. You played it. It's refreshing to meet an honest
man in Cuba. Like fresh air. I mean it! As I said, I just
handle security. You can't be too careful, Pal.'

9

Mr Stevens thought, 'There are two classes of people –
those who bother you with letters, and those that do
not.' He preferred postcards, and shot off fair fleets of
them, each as brief and perfect as a sonnet. Smoke signals
without pain, and stamps as pretty as the pictures, too.
He sent them from the good heart of America, from an
impulse, from Jefferson to Lincoln, and from ones who
send her hope: the darker heart eclipsed for now, a hood-
ed chandelier, closed cantina, in full tropic sun, which lit
new paths to wander, into the old town, *Habana Vieja*.
He looked at the stones, melting now beneath his feet.
Away they shone there! in the acute intelligence of their
own imagination. Imagination, don't let us down. Be your
    best,
your promise. *As if we spoke of light itself, of objects
and light. So, too, the mind adds nothing new – it adds
nothing, except itself*. He saw an endless procession
of new faces and, beneath every foot, a stone melting,
and every stone a moment coming, and from the sea
in new freshness and glosses, anointed with salt water.

He drank the air before him, as if all that was old was
new, and some were a poetry, all taking delight in its own
making lavish – as if of that *might be* it was truly made.

Heat

EVAN JONES

BUDDHA AND THE SOCIETY
OF JESUS

Anuradha, who entertained
the notion that his name
had led him willy-nilly to his lot,
endlessly pounded the concrete paths
of modern Anuradhapura
to enlighten however he could
tourists, pilgrims who walked to the great god Buddh'.

Nobody there was poorer
except perhaps the beggars resting in shade
to whom my daughter gave whatever she had
(she carried fruit; I gave her my small change
and a note or two perhaps of Monopoly money)
or the cattle moving the meadows in broad swathes.

I walked and chatted to the old man
(younger than me, as it turned out)
about this and that: archeology, changing times,
the ways of the world: who bows to whom,
how wives (and daughters) shop and talk –

it was a long, long walk
which finally left him drained.

Mostly we talked about what, alas,
scholars would call 'comparative religion.'
Schooling in Lanka is still run
mainly by the Society of Jesus
and my learned, weary, learned Buddhist man
who wants to give his knowledge free
(his notes are being made into a book:
he promised one to me)
at last conceded that my friends could pay
whatever it was worth
for further copies: 'Lanka needs the money'
(it has no lack of life).

I had foremost in mind my Jesuit master,
contemplative to a fault,
busy beyond belief:
their forces are no longer legion,
they try to cover the same territory:
there's this and that disaster –

but other mini-polymaths are eager too.

Bad news: a letter from my Buddhist pastor:
kidney trouble: hospital fees: the book's delayed
(the hospital fees are, say, three hundred Aussie bucks):

'thanks for the lovely gift'
of 'two modern poetry books.'
He has nothing left.

Now a new monster gives birth,
give what you can to Lanka:
they have them all, the deaf, the blind, the halt,
submissive, gentle, given to fate:

belief in God and gods covers a wide range.

Maybe Ganesh will thank you.

_____

Eureka Street

AILEEN KELLY

HIS VISITORS

They come at night, only a few,
membership pinned discreetly under the flap
of designer trek-shirt pockets.
No more studs, no leather or stiffened hair.
They rev and drag their new off-roaders,
and check for signal on their mobile phones.

Unregistered barrel and stock unlocked
from strongarm racks
under the halogens
wink at the tattered targets
and aim to do better, silenced by cellar walls.
A good mountain acre swallows the powder tang.

His mother's never about her cottagey garden.
Gone to New Zealand? Ballarat? Into a Home?
The fetid ivies
that month after month she poisoned and pulled
run ruthless again.
They reach up and suck out the light.

The Age

71

JOHN KINSELLA

THE VITAL WATERS

For Chris Hamilton-Emery, Robin Holloway, Tim, Alison, Tracy, Stephen,
Rod, John, Adam, Drew and Jeremy

About the asteroid belt of apples
fallen in the orchard,
leaves stacked up against the weight of micro-climates
and passers-by, the wind
untethers our lacunae,
touch-sensitive recollections
we get stuck in, where pleasure
is without extras,
and the swirl of components
makes anniversaries.

It looks benign, the Cam,
even in violent weather, it rides
only so high against the college stone,
threatens the bridge of sighs, the mathematical bridge
only so much; downriver, down below the lock,
residents of houseboats would say
it's rougher, the painted doors, thin bellies,
thrust against the backs, walking past,
you might imagine their overly sexual doings,
the smell of incense, the kaleidoscope of batik,
tough attitude to water rats; moving up to the Granta

the punts shovel indolence and suppressed excitement,
not quite strong enough poler hanging over the water,
an entire family rugged up against the cold;
the mud below pasture, cloister manuscript articled
anecdote; it all being alike there's no allegory,
only simile, which is not what you'd be led to think
drinking against Hobson, being surrounded by gas-tower
youth in the Grafton Centre; the resident population
left at taxi ranks while Trinity students
own the straight line and either side of it
from the Blue Boar home; only similes
as like to all the stones cobbled
in Saint John's where I often duck in for a piss
cutting through from Churchill to the Heffers bookshop,
or the Cambridge Health Food Shop, or even Sainsbury's
where recently in the absurdity of a metaphor, an employee
and a security guard held a patron hard to the floor,
his protesting 'Fuck off, I've done nothing wrong!'
walked around by those who don't want to know,
their *Guardians* tucked under arm, maybe a bottle of wine,
certainly Sainsbury's own brand hidden in double-layered
plastic bags; Erasmus hated the damp, Wittgenstein
had himself buried just behind Churchill, perpendicular
to the observatory where the actions of the sun
are noted by a famed astronomer and reported at High Table:
I like him crossing the Cam at Magdalene Bridge,
caught in the expanding gases of the sun,
a spot in time being a spot in the sun,

solar activity a field guide to form;
the Cam, sourced in Byron's Pool,
infiltrated by chemicals and the by-products
of Monsanto's genetic modification; did you know
there's a nuclear reactor in the middle of town?
Did you know they dismantle animals bit by bit,
glass windows to the hearts: it's the ultimate
house of pain – and the students generally speak
politely and marry the like-minded, attending
the odd poetry reading; in the bike throng, a pedestrian
hits the ground, come off the grass! By the grace of the senate
you wander in your gown, the university locked in a sense
of competitive fun with the *other* university, red brick
starting blocks a touch of Milton or those decadent
pre-Raphaelites; the DNA smorgasbord, the swans
served up in Benedictus benedicat, a touch of the gong,
and drinks in the senior combination room – that's where
I met Said and Vendler, Wilson Harris and a bunch of Nobel
Prize winners – Syd Barrett lives in his mother's old home;
son of a doctor, he wandered the banks of the Cam,
tripped in the Gog Magogs, grew intoxicated
in Wandlebury Wood – beetroot carrot aquaplane,
         hydrographer
tin cup, astronaut, and a theatre company loosening
the strings of a stratocaster, star fighter,
thin gypsum walls through which the utterances
of the Black Mountain School are heard; Syd Barrett's
history of art, preyed upon by video artists, village

idiots – them, not him – looking astonishingly
like Les Murray. Cambridge dishes out the kudos,
coughing up the loot; there are at least half a dozen
toilet blocks that make entries out of exits,
libraries that make scholars out of poets,
Australian Rules following faculty and students,
drunk on XXXX or Fosters, or cascading
through episodes of *Neighbours*,
a refutation that cultural studies
is yet to make its mark where the Pearl shines
out of the dead clasp; in the old court
a light shines out of *Macbeth*, a French horn
resonates through the stone, ivy turns
like a birthmark – spreading, yet fixed.

The growth of ancient stone at twilight
is sensed by one whose sight
is honed by the pulse of the river,
science of bridges, microcosm of pasture.

The riverlight feeds the roots of willows,
nettle spawn floats indolently on the vacation air:
the seasons are mixed here, and pheasants rise up out
of test crops, the pollen count low, heavy as shot;
Kipling makes Empire in the library
of Wimpole Hall, and throwing a whistleblower
a pound you damn history, fail to recall
that by agreement the ancient universities

survived the European war; runner-up to the VC's
medal for poetry back in the early nineteenth
century Wentworth's Australia was simulacrum,
really, in the non-jargon use of the word; our
Australian daughter became Cambridge at Park Street
Anglican-assisted school – she likes hymns in the morning.

Castle Hill remains indifferent to the breadth
of summer as back garden aviaries
burst with enthusiasm and small cars
parade themselves like a serenade;
the Gog Magog hills recline with sunset
and the child is able to say where she's
been and where she might go, mapping
from high ground as if all time has been taken.
Somewhere around here death broke
Hobson's girth, and this is what the drunk
reminds himself heading back home
after a riotous day in the Town & Gown,
and somewhere somebody refuses to age,
as the day condenses into an adage.

From Churchill, I most often cut through the orchard
of Saint Edmund's. The gardener there is a friend
by wave or single word, year after year, we trail
the seasons; he gave me the names of plants on
one occasion – our verbal moment; pigeons
and robins and squirrels work as a single

species below the hooded apple trees;
the windfalls before the ice comes
define the loss and presence,
the year gone but mid-year for some,
I cut through and past the fence lines,
past the barber's, up through Honey Hill,
past Euclid's indecision, the plimsoll line
of the university; the sanitary religious
vocation, theology against the minuscule
enclosed park where the Saturday craft market
titillates the tourists come by the gay pub
I cherish, though I don't drink, come by to sample
what was once the Jewish ghetto, and staring below
the reflective surface of the Cam, figure
this is where I'll come, so tempted by conversion
in this city-village-town based on primary numbers,
port and sherry, piss-ups and hashish in the gardens,
bears and college cats, cars forbidden during term,
forbidden to every Dr Faustus made in the cellars,
made in the dining halls, in rooms of the more modern
colleges where the heating vacillates, in lecture theatres
with pitted writing boards; in blue and brown books,
in oval windows and choirs sonorously out of control,
pretending restraint, pretending committees
keep the place together, that the Thatcher papers
are pivotal to the intestinal fortitude of the twentieth century.

The growth of ancient stone at twilight
is sensed by one whose sight
is honed by the pulse of the river,
science of bridges, microcosm of pasture.

Lion's Yard. Flashers. Sent Down.
Mould and watermarks, not far from the river.
Out to lunch. Iambic pentecostal.
Saints and serifs. Marxist extroverts
and infiltrators, anamarxist overlords,
cricketers and all shades of blue.
In the theatres they – we – watch art
dressed up as porn. Trinity
funds the poorer colleges.
At King's, revolutions are funded
only in part; the horse sculpture
has bolted from Jesus College; the Cam
is also a place for ducks, insects,
bank-dwelling rodents.

The growth of ancient stone at twilight
is sensed by one whose sight
is honed by the pulse of the river,
science of bridges, microcosm of pasture.

A splice of Milton's mulberry tree
grafts the bones of the Lindsays,
or the bones of Queenie

and her sharp conversationalism.
For eight years there were no anniversaries,
there weren't eight years and the anniversary
was a constant, hexes and nettles, bikes two abreast
down raceways, vivisectors who smile in passageways,
libraries that don't want books; their atheists
partially in the chapels, and light is the collation of factors,
as the silver oaks slice high winds, brighter than the moon
and its promise of choral interludes,
so brash in the dining rooms
when the rugby team has scraped home,
so obsessed with the retrievals of potlatch
and who has gone before – I deny prescience,
stolen spirits, dogs swimming the length
and breadth of Byron's pool – anything
can be re-created here, even the scorched
post-harvest Western Australian wheatbelt,
even the excesses of Silicon Valley.
Helen Vendler is said not to like Australian poetry –
generally, as a broader category – she is pleasant
to have a cool drink with in the refectory,
it's in the geology or geography but not necessarily
the genealogy; Empson's little desiring machines
have fortunately kept little out, though
it has its ways at interviews, class
wins out, and oh, in some places
nice arse – bottoms, as in summers we watch
in groups and classes *A Midsummer Night's Dream*

in the gardens – the folk from Heffers bookshop
on a rug of their own, downing champers – hi, Adam,
fellow Syd aficionado, who has heard the notorious
bootlegs, the copies of sessions few have ever heard –
sketches of a Cambridge childhood, tripping
on snippets of Shakespeare and the gibbet
on the crossroads; on Midsummer Common
the people against cruelty, the hemp foodists,
the vegan straight-edges: Strawberry Fair,
Cambridge – Pagan Festival . . . ?

On cowpat, grazing ground, long-haired overturf,
trance dance and hemp shirts, chai/tea tents
and guitar slayers, rude boys and Brisbane Hell's Angels,
'travellers,' solstice-gazers and academics
strolling in circuits, dogs, imitators, WASPs, the occasional
Catholic, dope-cloud makers and casual inhalers,
vicarious participants, ecstasy and acid purveyors,
potage with grudges, legitimate cases, dogs
with thick collars. Fight! Fight! News later,
a chest-stabber, victim rehabilitates
on the bouncy castle in kids' corner,
hooked drummers and Korg drivers, sorcerers
and preternatural shouters knowing self-worth,
self-love, empire food, dogs. Sky broods
though mud in abeyance, this year low
on wallow: a light shower, a sunset
to dampen prospect, just slightly, dogs

with bristling collars. Opening blue
twilight, trance dance centres. Loop,
scratch, boom box. Shout. The country
of vegans like the fifth voyage of Gulliver
and Stephen Rodefer collecting visuals
and gossip. Ankh and beads, beyond ecstatic,
flaps of cloth strung out by woofers,
O sonic boom box. Collect dance,
kids with collars, toes in the damp.
Hawk the cans. Bottles. Small pots
of amyl. Reggae tribes cross over
with ska-makers, vendors, hair-binders,
hot in the tent, pulsed and beaten,
whipped up slowly into bob and jump,
throwing ropes, flailing gunja-thick air.
Henna artists contract. Jar. Donor. Prayer,
Rodefer says: 'Only England can still get
truly medieval . . .' Sadistic piercers
and inscribers. Nervous handstanders
on guarana. Sex dance, trance dance, buzz.
Mumble, vibrating fingers, smoking implements
and lager, circus. Charms and spells
in blue and brown books, dogs, proofs
and magnets charged in the slam dance.

The growth of ancient stone at twilight
is sensed by one whose sight

is honed by the pulse of the river,
science of bridges, microcosm of pasture.

And Ted Hughes with the Addenbrookes nurse,
so crucify me to the breast-milk-drinking master
bilingual in the oak closets,
oh Monsanto, Monsanto you're on the way out,
crux of life empire-builders coring shires
and asset stripping nation, hedgehog light,
infused summer evening, French knickers
and jock straps in Lion's Yard, someone
throws up at a poetry reading; they closed
down the shelter run by ex-addicts
closed in and closed down –
under the bridge the rough sleepers
drop dead – all the time, dapper young men
and sharp young ladies (in Cambridge they
remain as such, no matter the linguistic
innovation), write smart articles
for *Varsity*, centring the culture.
Holy holy holy they worship
beside the off-licence, round church
Norman fetishes, rubbings
to pass the time where time is measured
subatomically – gangs of thieves work
the colleges, capricious around surveillance.
At Grantchester some of us listen
to Bikini Kill, in our heads,

beyond the reach of Monsanto.
Fuck you, Monsanto, fuck you.
Feed the poor, feed the earth?
Deniers, Monsanto, deniers.
Fuck it up. Good riddance,
and you're not the only player
in the anti-thinking school of Cambridge:
profit over ideas, and call it the new ethics,
where are the Leavisites when we don't
need them? Fin de fuck up.

The growth of ancient stone at twilight
is sensed by one whose sight
is honed by the pulse of the river,
science of bridges, microcosm of pasture.

The guitarist from Blur
made a Syd Barrett-inspired sculpture –
in the spirit of Cambridge – maybe –
he donated it to charity.
My head is lodged there.
It is a home. A cyclotron of language
that won't let up for a minute.
Part of me is in the infectious ward –
adult chickenpox – of Addenbrookes,
treated by the son of poet
Nathaniel Tarn – international ritualism
of Cambridge – hey, I owe you one,

good bloke that you seem to be
in the ward of sweat and peyote.
The Wellcome trust spreads its wings –
there's an early Black Sabbath cult there.
Mice that grow ears – human ears,
and dogs that bark backwards.
See how words demean context.
Blood on the floor, protest.
It is summer, and yet so cold
at night we huddle under the blankets.
'You Australians are always
on about the weather . . . '

The growth of ancient stone at twilight
is sensed by one whose sight
is honed by the pulse of the river,
science of bridges, microcosm of pasture.

Meanjin

ZOLTAN KOVACS

GHOSTS

Archaeologists have found
   In the Severn Estuary's grey
   Expanse of silty mud,
   Footsteps firm as yesterday's
   Three thousand years old.

A child's, a woman's, a man's,
   Striding, pausing, turning,
   Unaware their innocent caravan
   Would be recorded by a tide
   Filling up the pan

Of their heels and arches, toes,
   With a soft care of sediment.
   Fifteen paces each (or so)
   With nothing to say what sent
   Them out that way, who chose

The errand, what intent, whether
   It was simply play.
   But I know who they are: brother,
   Sister, son, wife, sage,
   Hunter, poet, clerk, mother,

Father, painter, astronauts,
   Cocklers, potters, futurists:
   Child, woman, man: all ghosts
   Like me. Not fatalists,
   Optimists, the footprints boast.

Famous Reporter

ANTHONY LAWRENCE

WANDERING ALBATROSS

It's as though the Continental Shelf, with its east-facing rifts
    and cliffs
were visible; as though the full-bodied waves that blow over it,
freighted with kelp, tidewood, and the bloated bodies of dead
    seals
were thermals, sideways tracking and printed with spirals
that mark a slow convergence of warm
and nutrient-rich cold water.
   What rides this marriage of elements
     does so with a wingspan
hammered from great distances, its feathers containing
worn emblems and fading lines, such as might be found
within the pages of a passport when travel was slow,
when destinations involved a leaving of smoke
and waterlines while crossing the world's oceans.

Breeding and exhaustion are this wanderer's only reasons,
in all weathers and seasons, for flight.
Coming in from the South, it angles away and down,
almost wetting the tip of its leeward wing
before raking a dimpled current line
for upwellings of cuttlefish, chrome-plated splinters
of schooling sauri, or a sampling from its own reflection,

which it swallows, saltwater
being an elixir for this long-range survivor.

And when, after days of gliding, its hollow bones
take on the ache of being all at sea,
it will follow a ship, inspecting it for mast wires,
an unpeopled railing, for anything upon which to perch.

To find a mate, the females gather on barren outcrops
surrounded by suitors, each one
expectant and competitive in the sleek,
wind-tailored plumage of their kind.
    Having found each other,
        they remain at the centre
of the cycles of company and separation
for up to eighty years, despite long absences,
despite their differences.

See them coming in – white gliders with landing gear
that paddles for purchase on the stones
of sub-Antarctic islands where their mates are waiting,
alike and yet unique, their singular scents and calls
dividing a raucous field with welcome.
    One partner. One life, together.
        And for every egg that grows
and breaks under terrible weather, a fledgling will emerge
to test its wings and stand its ground
for nine months, then leave to circle the globe,

solitary in its preparations for love,
the sensory avatars of sea and air
made manifest in the compass glass of its eyes.

Australian Book Review

GEOFFREY LEHMANN

THIRTEEN LONG-PLAYING HAIKU

I

A cigarette stuck to his lips,
at night the amateur broadcaster
washes his precious vinyl LPs
in warm soapy water,
and coughs himself to sleep.

Next day the needle
sticks in the grooves
and his voice is a croak on air.

II

Small silver discs whose binary code
is read by a ruby laser
obsess my days and nights,
colourful illustrations in their jewel cases,
and sleeve note stories
of Ravel walking along the beach
at Monte Carlo,
Brahms's hopeless love for Clara.

III

Our demographic:
aged over 50, male.
Some buy numerous versions of a single piece,
others – 'completists' – want
a composer's every work.
Some study ratings in guides for hours,
want no repeats in their collection
and insist on original instruments.
Others go crazy at sales
and emerge from an orgasm of spending
loaded with CDs,
blinking in the sunlight.

IV

I replace Allegri *after* Alkan.
I'd forgotten
there was a double 'l' in Allegri.

V

Members of a masonic order
standing apart from wives and partners
we furtively exchange information
about bargains and rarities.
As our collections grow
we abandon the mainstream,
and develop bizarre tastes.

VI

Some of us file composers
in alphabetical order,
and have systems
for filing within a composer.
Alphabetists avoid compilations.
Do you file
the string quartets of Debussy and Ravel
under D or R?

VII

'Where's *Einstein on the Beach*?'
the free-filers ask their overflowing
and continually circulating collections,
stacked under beds, in broom cupboards,
discs piled in drawers
and detached from their jewel cases.
For a week Philip Glass hides
between Louis Armstrong in Paris
and Monteverdi's *Orfeo*,
then moves on and finds new companions.

VIII

The older dealers understand their clients.
A woman is buying *Figaro* for her daughter:
'Isn't Mozart a bit light?'
'Madam,

is the ceiling of the Sistine Chapel "a bit light"?'
Wrapping my purchase,
he diagnoses me
through Henry Kissinger glasses:
'If you can't make up your mind what to play,
play your collection
in alphabetical order.'

IX

Arriving home at night
with my newspaper neatly
folded under my arm,
I'm bailed up by my son
at the top of the stairs:
'Mum, he's hiding more CDs
in his *Financial Review*.'

X

Driving a carload of young women
to a tax class I'm giving,
I turn the ignition key.
Will I switch off John Cage's
Sonatas and Interludes for Prepared Piano?
I let the CD play unannounced
and roll back the sunroof.
The car fills with sunlight and young women's conversation
punctuated by strange and luminous percussions.

Gulls and the grey arch of Sydney's Harbour Bridge pass
    over us.
They thank me as we park:
'That was very pleasant.'

XI

A second-hand music shop
leaves a message on my voicemail.
Within minutes I'm sorting through
thousands of baroque and early music CDs.
'A deceased estate,
he was a baroque man – '
they quote an amateur broadcaster's name.
'I'm a baroque man too,' I say.
But not like this,
every little byway explored,
volumes of duets for recorders,
lute music that would play for weeks,
lovingly assembled
by a narrow and exact mind.
Shaken, I buy just some Ockeghem and Handel.

At home I open a jewel case and smell ash –
the dead man's cigarettes.
'Dad,' the voices say,
'it'll happen to you – to your collection.'

XII

The collector writes his own valedictory:
'We approve
how you studiously play
almost every CD you buy.
We forgive the occasional omission,
one or two missed in a boxed set of Schubert lieder,
and those you never play, but love
as a memento
of the same performance on much played vinyl.
We admire your urge to know and experience
blues, minimalism, a capella masses,
Alkan to Zelenka – even Broadway musicals.
The collector's life is solitary and odd,
his assembly of objects
meaningful only to himself.'

XIII

I'm tipping CDs into the 10 stack
in the boot of my red car,
constructing my new identity:
Handel's *Saul*, Schnittke's concerto grosso,
some John Lee Hooker,
Lou Reed's *Transformer* –
some of the dead broadcaster's treasures,
his Buxtehude La Capricciosa variations.
I'm also removing my old self,
replacing the discs in their cases.

I have the jewel cases laid out
like a neurosurgeon's instruments,
as I withdraw and insert,
fingertips gingerly holding each disc by its edge,
checking each label is up.
Tonight I'm driving to a beach house
three hours of tunnels and freeways,
past dairy country,
through eucalypt forests
and along a moonlit peninsula,
the music and the road
a single line of thought.

Heat

KATHRYN LOMER

TIBETAN WINDHORSE

And then the bees are gone
from oregano air; swifts depart.
Night begins in afternoon
and we withdraw to a mind-set of rooms.
X-ray days expose skeletons:
in my garden a bonsai pomegranate
splits its sides with pink glass beads
and figs try turning purple before the snow.
Persimmon lanterns up the street
throw light on ripening olives.
My Greek neighbours pine:
Let them come to us for gods.
Mornings are always dark
and short days make narrow bones;
all the rings on my fingers shift.
Gales toss bull kelp onto Bass Strait shores,
glass shatters, and roofs lift from lives.
Our *koi-nobori* leaps and leaps
among the figs; going back is too hard.
I remind myself it's also a time of rainbows
and think to fly five coloured ribbons
from the stick-like Red Delicious.
My makeshift windhorse flags

answers and as I watch its mad dance
something settles. When I look again
the last hard fig is caught
among new shoots and the light
stays a little longer.

Southerly

JENNIFER MAIDEN

THUNDERBOLT'S WAY

And who was Yellow Long?
Thunderbolt's Way weds Uralla to Gloucester.
At an Armidale workshop, a fine
blonde woman writes of Slessor being
ruined day by day working for
Frank Packer and tells how she watched
this happen as a young reporter. I admire
her writing style and think:
how 1960s-eager she'd have been
then, and suggest she write
her anecdote about a Christmas tree
she made for the office – how Slessor
seemed strained, unused to gifts, in
her poem. She's reluctant, for fear
of being thought 'a star-fucker.' I
wonder if that whole 'star-fucking' thing
against poetry's not a way to inhibit
analysis's historic inhabitation. Anyhow,
                            discussing writing
about Thunderbolt, my daughter
                        says I'd be accused
of star-fucking him. So let's discuss
the real stars first: when one

drives Thunderbolt's Way in the dark,
                    they are
like all else there very close: not
larger but closer, the treetops, the hills,
the past: the shadow past that looms
and glooms like a mountain. And who
was Yellow Long? Two women, both
part Aboriginal, or one
             called Mary Anne, to whom
 he was faithful until her death.
                          There is no history
which agrees on her identity. A century
and a half ago, the snow
here fell bitter in winter.
Over there, you can see Slessor,
as he did often, hide
in a host's library to avoid
the country scenery, over there
in my black driving brain. One day
weary Thunderbolt rode down
to a cottage and told its lady
his woman was dying nearby, by a cave.
The lady drove her cart and brought
Yellow Long to the house to die. Louisa
or Mary Anne? Louisa
was married to a shepherd, Cranky Bob,
and Mary Anne was Thunderbolt's wife
for years herself a bushranger, who

had three children, was imprisoned
twice for vagrancy, released
by Parliament, which ever
loves best, like Queen Victoria
a good romantic story. The family
verson leaves out Louisa. I wonder
what the death certificate gives
as her name, apart from that it cites
lung inflammation, which was perhaps
TB from prison. And anyway in life
how close the stars, the treetops, the cold
mountain to the crisp cave bed at dawn.
Nothing worse here ever perhaps than what
Packer did to Slessor slower, or what
the fear of star-fucking does. And who
                         was Yellow Long?
What happened to the other who was gone?
Some report the body in the photo,
post postmortem, not at
his best, wasn't him:
Fred Ward or Thunderbolt but his half brother
or yet another Thunderbolt, who
escaped with Fred early from Cockatoo
Island. So maybe Louisa
related to one of them and not the star.
The real stars are close not large, the road
from Uralla to Gloucester would worry Slessor:
it is direct but climbs far

through forests and mountains that seem
to walk by your side and are gone
not so much numb as near, like history,
                              and then who on
this night earth was Yellow Long?

_____

Southerly

LES MURRAY

TRAVELLING THE BRITISH ROADS

Climb out of medieval one-way
and roundabouts make knotted rope
of the minor British roads
but legal top speed on the rocketing
nickel motorway is a lower limit!
I do it, and lorries howl past me.

Sometimes after brown food
at a pub, I get so slow
that Highland trackways
only have one side
since they are for feet
and hoofs of pack horses
and passing is ceremony.

Nor is it plovers
which cry in the peopled glens
but General Wade's chainmen
shouting numbers for his road
not in the Gaelic scores
but in decimal English.

Universal roads return as shoal
late in the age of iron rims.
Stones in the top layer to be
no bigger than would fit in your mouth,
smiles John MacAdam. *If in doubt*
test them with your lips!

Highwaymen, used to reining in
thoroughbreds along a quag of track,
suddenly hang, along new carriageways,
or clink iron on needy slave-ships,
but waggon horses start surviving
seven years instead of three
at haulage between new smoke towns.

The railways silence the white road.
A horseman rides along between villages;
the odd gig, or phaeton;
smoke and music of the *bosh*
rising out of chestnut shade:
Gypsies, having a heyday.
Post roads, drying out, seem strange
beaches, that intersect each other.

When housemaids uncovered their hair
at windows, and a newfangled
steamroller made seersucker sounds
there were swans on the healed canal,

and with the sun came the Queen's
Horse Artillery in tight skeleton coats
to exercise their dubbined teams
watched by both fashionable sexes
in bloomer-like pedal pants.

I knew to be wary of the best dressed,
decent with the footsore,
but frontier-raffish with all
because the scripts they improvised from
were dry and arch, but quickly earnest.

From that day, and the audible
woodwind cry of peafowl, it was half
a long lifetime till jerked motors
would ripple the highroad
with their soundwaves, like a palate,
and kiss its gravel out
with round rubber lips
growling for the buckets of tar

and another life to the autobahn
nothing joins, where I race the mirror
in a fighter cockpit made posh
under flak of Guy Fawkes eve
over the cities of fumed brick.

Meanjin

JOYCE PARKES

PROPINQUITY'S PREMISE
(For C.H.)

'Thank you for the life,' meanings
including adieux and accents,
with mentions of salubrious events/

issues containing contentions of
cages and caiques. While trades
and traditions wonder if the sun's

hours are there to arrest time
or to assign chequered moments
to action, freedom of speech

spans contradiction, summonses
scorers and saunterers to festival
stations, while work leans on time

and writing defines definitions,
filing the volition that learning,
like loving, cannot stop for long.

Overland

DOROTHY PORTER

ODE TO AGATHA CHRISTIE

Is this the crucial clue?
The bug-like trilobite
I bought from a slippery gypsy
in Prague,
still staring through its crystalline eyes
from the floor of an extinct sea.

I am spooked
by the abysmal depths
of my own life's mystery.
Like a belly-up Christie village
I'm nipped by the red herrings
of every pyrrhic victory.

Can I pocket and know this sunset
flaring over the rollers
of the cold Bass Sea?
No photograph, no poem
will make it anything
but a stillborn cliché.

Is murdering time
the most true and convincing
perfect crime?

I tangle in the plot
chasing the hit-and-run driver
of my careless past tense.

Why does my childhood swimming pool
now stagnate darkly
behind a high wire fence?

I rub my clever egg head
and show off my waxed
moustache.
O Agatha, what fun playing
Poirot
to douse my fear in farce!

But how can I make
my solution ship arrive?
To what shimmering port
will it take me?
Or is it just an easy exile
from blind faith and wishful talk?

Death Comes As The End –
Agatha, you threw out cosy
when you served up dread.

As surely as my trilobite
with the right time, place
and gritty clout,
may I be preserved
as insoluble enigma
when a killer comet snuffs me out.

Heat

Philomena van Rijswijk

MY BEAUTIFUL WHITEWASHED SKIN

When you wake in the night
you hear a high-pitched whine
that, in some places in the world,
is called the singing of the stars.
Other places, it's called loneliness.
And yet in others, it's mortality.

I wake, and I luxuriate
in the perfect fit of my aloneness.
Yes, to have my skin on is a luxury.
In spirit, I have whitewashed the ancient
timber walls of my selfhood.
I have painted fresh medallions of
makebelieve flowers on the membranous panels.
The winter rains, the churlish equinoctial winds,
once deflowered them. No more.

The walls of my home are decorated and impenetrable.
I have canted a curse.
I have made my celibate skin into a celebration.
No one need admire the clever handiwork,
the pleasing symmetry.

No uxoriousness is demanded,
merely,
this unctuous containment.
This healing liniment that fingertips
the lineaments of my salvation. This salve.

I live in a cleft not reached by roads.
There is barely any mail.
My beautiful, whitewashed wholeness is my home.

Hecate

PETER ROSE

QUOTIDIAN

Summer and open doors.
Sore throats dry as cepous tanks.
Serpents multiply, worrying about –
not language this time but how
to holiday in a figurative skin.
Before collapse the condition
must be beautiful. Extraneous noises
whether burglar or rodent rattling a pane
bring exchange students seeking
not verification this time
but something to open the wine.
We stammer and splutter
and soar through the roof.
Traffic shuffles its pack.
Manuscripts mate in the rushes –
Adored Allergies, *Everyman's Book of Incest*.
Lifting carpets they bring us
booty from a bombed Society.
Acrid are those air-conditioned rumours:
her voice quite shot above the stave.
A clinician's sleek phrasing.
Jars of lemon butter
which a grandmother saved.

Or so they said, and open doors.
I remember her vaguely
but not her condiments,
only someone removing her dentures
as in a morality play. We visit
the dead with appalled compliments,
testing upholstery. What frightened me
across that still acre,
everyone's portcullis down?
Panic marches on parliament
giving interviews. On television
the febrile conductor
dies for hourly bulletins,
serial ravages mining his brow,
but they go out with rutting pandas
and the theme from *Hair*.
Summer and open doors.

Meanjin

CRAIG SHERBORNE

JOURNO

My desk's across from Racing.
I'm Murders-Paedophiles-Falls From Grace
who bellow back through a fly-screen
while my pen wags across the page: I make
stick figures without limbs,
a foot with a snapped leg,
half an arm, three fingers
bent back, splayed.
I have no second language
unless you count these stumps
of words I use, scratches
and splinters on shorthand paper.
At first glance a sheet of music
but with all the notes broken.

My hand's a plastic telephone.
I shoulder it kinked against my ear,
top lip kissing the speaker dots.
Grievers refuse to talk to me
but 'I'm sorry for your loss' is enough
to finesse their heavy, thank-you breath –
the elocution of trust.

For comment, Professors of Everything begin
their quotes with the usual 'Sad.'

I wait for the dead to happen.
'That's why it's called a deadline,'
I yawn to the new girl,
like showing off a callous, a scar.
She frowns admiringly.
She's never seen a corpse but wants to.

***

Quadrant

Peter Steele

VERMEER'S GEOGRAPHER

From the gilded air of Dutch imagining, light
    falls and falls upon him. Nothing –
not, for sure, the lean belly of curtain,
    or the diked glass matching his framing –
can play him false, there with poised dividers,
    mind abristle before its maze.

Of course, there is always the world, putting its case
    for bluff and rarefaction, schist
when least called for, lava's pitiless cream,
    the clove reek of Spice Islands,
throb on tundra, the hushed spill of grasses.
    Better than you or I, he knows,

young as he is, that atlas, globe, and map
    patching the wall are paired with cloth
at his table's edge – flaired, crumpled, unfinished,
    apt for touching, never one's own,
something of ocean lifting away from the surface,
    the whole if at all pointed elsewhere.

The Australian

HUGH TOLHURST

SOME MUSIC IN THE CHIESA SAN CARLINO

The Geminiani has a gamin beauty, tilting
over the aged marble, misbehaving notes
play about Borromini's radical diamond space.
And it is a young music, the players maybe
twenty years of age maybe less. You can hear
youth in these strings, it's in the pauses
which smack of the same quality, the same
engaging nervousness, as the smiles which
punctuate long Italian introductions. Well,
as the programma moves on through Sibelius,
it's pretty well the one smile, the Spanish
smile from the second violins, the Spanish
smile in cascading brushed notturno, her wit
glinting as an enraged Roman motorist adds
brass to Vivaldi's allegro. In the words
of the Presidente e Direttore Artistico, these
players whose more significant minority is not
Mediterranean but Asian (the handsome dude,
rear of first violins, even in Penguin suit
looks only slightly more Japanese than punk),
these chamber strings of Melbourne are important.
And of course, as the ambassador pulls his beard

and leaves, the listener must agree. Your aged
expatriate charms survived the cute viola who
recalled you wry request of Bruce Dawe last
Writers' Fest: your evening is a romanza of pizza
while already waiting on Telecom Italia. Her
name's Melita, she's from Balwyn and her desire
involves clubbing with the Romans.

_____

Quadrant

JOHN TRANTER

TRANSATLANTIC

Paris was not a place, it was the event,
and in that event the great writer
wrote about her grand obsession: herself.
Remember that the great writer liked
the evening telephone. The fade of age.

She said snob strongly and snob often,
that was what she wanted.
If you go to the reading-rooms
as a result of smoking the herb of contempt
nothing you read will do you any good.
Why am I talking to you?

We received at least the evening sky
which was hers to inherit; that,
and a few thousand dollars.

My friendships after all, Helene said,
were based on direct emotion.
She did not stifle the great writer,
rather the work of the great writer
stifled others, a known council of vulgarisers.
You are journalists, Helene said,

you are all mechanical men.
Helene would be more inclined to violence, and
these *femmes de ménage* stumbled into
a life filled with permanent anger.
Naturally it is a big explosion,
she yelled. You remember emotions.

The great writer had a mystic in to teach us
mysticism. He was attracted by Janet.
Drop dead, Janet said. So he taught
moral tales, how ambition clogs the career.
Discretion is a kid of dilution, courtesy a limp.

O far shore, wrote the voice.

They met in the Luxembourg Gardens and
paperback in hand, turned to rend
what was left of my love story –
those dark intellectual comments,
later printed in the *Moral Tales*.

There were traces in the enormous room
of what had made them.
Just stay here. We spent hours there.
To have him lain with a little book.

O drink, bring peace to the flesh.

CHRIS WALLACE-CRABBE

FROM THE ISLAND, BUNDANON

I

Eight stones lie on my trestle desk,
three cream-striped with injected quartzite,
one a very plain grey segment
for the moon goddess, three pebble-sized
white, ginger and lustrous black; the last
a pocked palmful of sandstone.
River-rubbed, they fall into design.

II

Muscular underachievers with big brainpans,
Neanderthals dawdled on in the west of Europe
until that corner caught up with the rest of us,
then nicked on smartly, ahead for centuries
or more, playing tricks with bright metal and glass.
Where are the old values?
What became of those big blokes and their women.

III

Unknowable, they fall into design,
stars that all peoples have known

by cluster-name, and flowing down the sky
a Milky Way: the whole beyond belief,
altogether impossible,

      yet across them drags
the flickering of two planes bound for Melbourne.

IV

Why is mistletoe so droopingly widespread
in this country, so far indeed
from Sir J.G. Frazer's multinational magic?
Is it a marsupial kissing-bough
trailing its tressage of scimitars and bullets
in parody on a parent eucalypt?
The bush is hospitable to such festoons.

V

The rocksolid wombat
that has a dithering habit
neither thunders away
nor gets around to diving
into his well-dug bolthole
but pauses in dusty fur
to consider all the options.

VI

Urban *they* remain quite as desiccating
as the dear little sachet of calcium chloride

you find in a chemist's bottle.

                                  They
have no response to the way the lower
squadron of windblown cloud
rushes past us, dynamically indifferent
to the marbled welkin above.

VII

Innocent cylinder with a wound,
you have kept the grape's rich blood
from the disillusioning breath of day
at your own cost. Freckled and branded
you lie here on the table,
one end pale magenta. Far from your tree
you became pleasure's sacrifice.

VIII

Scar tissue earned from shorts and dead lantana
mapping that stony island
has left a cartography of signs
all over both shins, generously so.
Like stars or complicated cells
they look to spell a meaning I can't read,
inescapably riverine.

                            And rough.

IX

To make, said Hardy, the clock of years
turn backward, I might enter then
a decade where there was my father
and I could know my eldest son
in his plight, but these are dream
as I shuffle the stones on my writing desk
and the stars whirl in endless night.

Meanjin

Fay Zwicky

MAKASSAR, 1956

We didn't fly the homeland in those days.
Lumbering P & O Orient liners slid sedately off
to postwar bliss in England; we spoke with English
vowels, revered our teachers, grieved for Hamlet
and the star-crossed lovers.
Parents, relatives and friends cried and waved,
the streamers strained, snapped, collapsed
in lollypop tangles on the wharf. Pulling away
from the tumbled web, we didn't care about
falling behind, getting ahead, dry-eyed and
guiltless, went as everything was happening
somewhere else. I wouldn't have seen the signs.

Mine was someone else's colonial route,
heading for the magic islands learnt from Conrad.
I took instead a trampy old Dutch steamer,
the *Nieuw Holland* plying the spicy archipelago
for Koninklijke Paketvaart Maatschappij, the
Royal Packet Navigation Company: wood-slatted cabin doors,
cork-chequered mats in *Badkamers*, tin dippers,
tubs for dousing, cold water tasting salty, three green
bottles in the toilet: paper was for infidels.

Decks buzzed with students going home, new
graduates from our Colombo Plan, old hands from
what was called The Indies in *tempo dulu*, stiff-backed
older lady teachers, nurses like grey Mrs Marshall from
Ballarat who'd been in prison camp and knew the ropes.
Mr Tisnadi Wiria with his wife, four children; Som and
Suparpol, the plump Thai dentists; shiny avuncular Mr Doko,
cultural superintendent from North Bali and pretty Enni
from Kadiri. And big-boned Mrs Stecklenburg with a
Victory Roll and pale apologetic daughter – the way
that woman sang! We all got into the act but respectful,
celebrating all hours and lining up for nasi goreng,
flower-cut beetroot, lobster-men, oranges and apples
for our games. The ship's lights caught us frolicking
in their benign glare.

Mornings found the sharp-nosed Aussie horse trainer,
Mr Young, rakish-angled felt hat bound for Singapore.
He used to take a daily turn around the deck, smashing
his thin Malayan wife against the rails like a rag doll.
She never made a sound. We heard he had horses and a cockatoo
on board. Later, in shock I watched her hurl a dipper
against the bathroom wall, weeping. She lived what I
had only seen on stage or read about in penny novels,
what my Nana called 'hot stuff': other peoples' lives.
Betrayal, death and homicidal rage were opera.
It must have flicked my mind to wonder how you stuck
with someone slamming your bones on what passes for

a normal morning walk, stay silent, letting it happen
over and over. Marriage, after all, meant love, an infinity
of calm water shining for miles under a new moon,
our kindly southern stars. My thoughts were virtuous,
naive, each nerve geared to heartless young imaginings,
how much better I would do it.

I ate a poisoned oyster on the Brisbane stop,
puked the north-east coast as far as the Arafura Sea.
Jovial Dr Chi's bulk filled my tiny cabin as he poked
my gut with some contempt: 'Gas, my girl, just gas!'
Offended, I lay flattened for a day, revived with Chinese
powders of a suspect green, began a letter to my mother,
tore it up: my life or what I thought was called a life
had just been launched, the world my oyster.
Never let them know and don't give up.
Dolphins and flying fish leaped and soared in the wake.
Hypnotised in hazy warmth, we dozed the afternoons
away and nightly watched Orion shift his shape.

The night before Makassar Mr Doko sang a song from Timor
about an Australian soldier with an Indonesian girlfriend.
Hearing he's been wounded by the Japanese
she rushes off to find him, takes him to the hospital
where he dies of wounds. The tears were in our eyes
for such devotion. The girl then dresses in a soldier's
uniform, goes off to fight and gets killed too. How I
remember how we listened, how it cast us into unexpected

silence, grieving for the two young star-crossed lovers.
Mr Doko beamed with pride in his song and its effect.
Mr Eisenring looked impatient, Mr Nasiboe folded his hands:
they were getting off in the morning.

I woke to calm, the shuddering engines stopped and
through the cabin porthole saw the sea, flat, metallic,
sage-green, the ship becalmed as if in oil, still as a dream.
On deck, the soft rain fell, spindly palms fringed the
shoreline, little prahus and rowing boats swished
silently between the harbour's knolls, each marked with
a coconut palm or two just like the comic strips.
Steady rain fell on the upturned faces of the children
dotted red and yellow, blue and green waving from the wharf,
skinny arms outstretched for oranges and apples we threw.
Any minute now we'd be on land. I couldn't wait.

Boys scampered under giant banana leaves held dripping
above their heads, darting and calling. Steel-helmeted
young militia men lounged near our enchanted ship,
rifle-bayonets slung casually over one shoulder, smooth
and nerveless features gazing past us: boy-men so they seemed.
I'd never seen a gun and felt no fear: just something else
we'd read about at home. Our fathers used them in the War.
It would never happen again, we said.

After the unloading of the flour, each lumpy bag carted
down the gangway by a tribe of scrawny men, legs bowed

under the weight, scrambling fast like a moving spider's nest,
we were let out. Through Imigrasi and the stampings, permits,
questions, then released into the rain, the fragrant air
of frangipani, coconut oil, clove-scented Kretek cigarettes.
Blue smoke rose from street corner braziers charring
kambing saté sticks: our senses reeled and charged,
the crowd milling, jostling us into town while Mr Eisenring
and Mr Nasiboe disappeared for ever in a heap of luggage,
gesticulating porters and two burdened *betjaks*.

A wedding procession threaded its way along
Djalan Pintu Dua at a fine clip, embroidered silks
and gold-fringed parasols, crimson, blue and green.
First came a tall big drum, bicycle attached, the
pedals dangling from the skin, its rider thumping
forward, trombone, flutes and trumpets blaring.
My heart stood open like a door – the bride looked
very nervous sitting, eyes downcast, beside her thin
proud groom in a little cart bringing up the rear.
As it jolted past us in the warm rain, I felt a poem
starting to take shape under the reedy rhythms of the band.
It settled on my heart for nearly fifty years.

Later, looking up the Indonesia-Inggeris pocket
dictionary given me by Fong Chi Hang as I sheltered
from the driving rain in his Shanghai Sport Shop, the
phrase 'the West Monsoon' was rumoured. Can't remember how
I got to be out back eating a soup of fermented rice

and octopus with Mr Fong, his wife and lots of curious
kids or how I came to have his dictionary.
Must have needed a word for how I felt and looked up
'happy' announced 'Saja senang hati' while everybody laughed.
But I was relishing the darkened vowels, the alien softness
that spelled out my state however topsy-turvy it might be.
For once sound matched sense.

'Bahagian' was happiness and as I spoke the word,
three women passed in purdah in the street, thickly veiled
from head to toe in black like mourners. Their burning eyes
arrested me, speaking soundless of an older, fiercer order
of things. Haunted eyes that followed me in dreams – I see
them still – their black concealment hinting how
it's possible to be in one place, also somewhere else,
possible to let things happen over and over, possible
to stick in silence to pain's colours and, if it's in you,
transmit poems: burning, angry, frightened, loving, yearning
poems, rock-grooved water poems, poems of flame and
moon-flute poems, poems of the ocean and volcano's crater,
poems repeating dreams from darkness, remembering
    darkness.

Never in my life had I been so near to growing up
as on that day in Makassar back in 1956 watching
a wedding in the rain and the women passing.

Heat

CONTRIBUTORS' NOTES

BRUCE BEAVER was born in the Sydney seaside suburb of Manly on 14 February, 1928. He was one of Australia's greatest poets, widely admired for his unique and extensive contribution to Australian literature. The author of thirteen volumes of poetry, Beaver's voice was wide-ranging and international in scope, while retaining a clearly Australian stance and style. Beaver's many honours include the Patrick White Award in 1982; the Christopher Brennan Award in 1983; a New South Wales Literary Citation honouring him for his 'unique and valuable contribution to Australian literature' in 1990; and an Honorary Doctorate from the University of Sydney, awarded posthumously in 2004. Bruce Beaver died in the early hours of 17 February 2004 after a long illness. His posthumous collection of poems, *The Long Game and Other Poems*, was published by University of Queensland Press in 2005.

JUDITH BEVERIDGE was born in England in 1956 and came to Australia in 1960. She has published three books of poetry, most recently *Wolf Notes* (Giramondo, 2003) which won the 2004 Judith Wright Calanthe Award for Poetry, and the Victorian Premier's Prize for Poetry. She is also the 2005 recipient of the Philip Hodgins Memorial Medal for excellence in Literature. She is the poetry editor of *Meanjin*.

About 'The Shark' Beveridge writes: 'This poem belongs to a series of poems I'm writing about fishermen and the sea. In composing the poem I was largely driven by sound. Wallace Stevens makes the comment that sometimes in writing poetry it is necessary to by-pass the intellect and that one of the best ways of doing this is through music. I found that by concentrating on the repetitions of certain consonants and vowel sounds in the poem, the content more or less revealed itself. The poem went through less drafts than normal as the form revealed itself to me fairly early on.'

JAVANT BIARUJIA is a poet of mixed Celtic and Mediterranean descent, living in Melbourne. He has recently published two books, *Calques* and *Low/Life*, the latter shortlisted in 2003 for The Age Book of the Year prize. A Dutch translation of his play *Comfort* premiered this year in The Hague.

About 'Icarus' Biarujia writes: 'The poem, which belongs to an as yet unpublished book-length collection titled *Virilities*, is a loose reinterpretation of the Icarus myth. (As such, the first person subject pronoun could perhaps also be read as an initial capital letter.) Written in a reflective, diary-like style, the poem is a disquisition on freedom, responsibility and mortality I find difficult to explain further, except perhaps through the words of another poem: "I love psychological analysis but practise catharsis interruptus . . . . The imagination is the point, where . . . I forget the currents, finding my own level, *above* and *below* consciousness. Poetry, like water, is necessary for life to flourish . . . . Without poetry, we are *deluded*; we should surely grow older earlier" ("Being, Its Own Reward").'

MTC CRONIN's tenth book of poetry is <*More or Less Than*> *1–100* (Shearsman Books, UK, 2004). Her 2001 book, *Talking to Neruda's Questions*, has recently appeared in a bilingual Spanish/English edition (Safo, Chile, 2004) and will appear in Italian translation (by Hans Kitzmuller) in late 2005 (Britain,

Italy). A selected poems, *The Ridiculous Shape of Longing*, will shortly be published in Macedonian, Bosnian, Croatian and Serbian (Blesok, Macedonia, 2005). Her next collection is forthcoming with Ravenna Press, USA.

About 'The Dust in Everything' Cronin writes: 'Dust! It's both a gently soft and theatening word. It's beautiful – quite poetic in itself – and also represents the ultimate disintegration of our human bodies. I was watching a program on TV about how everything in the universe (and perhaps all universes) is made up of the same basic elements. Star dust and stones and siderites and scissors. Fruit, forks, feathers and flame. All share composition. As do we. My poem, "The Dust in Everything,' uses dust as a metaphor for what everything has in common: that all seems to eventually disappear yet nothing can really go anywhere (because it's all part of everything). Sort of metaphysical yet not at all really. You dust by unsettling dust and the dust just settles. There is no escape – even to dust. But understanding why is to be comforted by inclusion.'

BRUCE DAWE is widely recognised as Australia's most popular poet. Born in 1930 in Fitzroy, Victoria, he worked in a variety of occupations before retiring from the University of Southern Queensland in 1992 when he was appointed their first Honorary Professor. After successfully completing two Masters degrees and a PhD he was awarded honorary degrees from the University of Southern Queensland and the University of New South Wales. Other awards include the Ampol Arts Award for Creative Literature (1967), Grace Leven Poetry Prize (1978), Braille Book of the Year (1979), Myer Poetry Prize (1965, 1968), Patrick White Literary Award (1980), Christopher Brennan Award (1984), Paul Harris Fellowship of Rotary

International (1990), Order of Australia (AO) for his contribution to Australian literature (1992), the inaugural Philip Hodgins Medal for Literary Excellence (1997), Australia Council for the Arts Emeritus Writers Award for his long and outstanding contribution to Australian literature (2000) and a Centenary Medal (2003). Dawe has published thirteen books of poetry, one book of short stories, one book of essays, four children's books and has edited two other books. His collected poems, *Sometimes Gladness*, was named by the National Book Council as one of the ten best books published in Australia in the previous ten years.

About 'Othernesses Other Than Our Own' Dawe writes: 'I wrote this poem while returning on the Indian Pacific from Perth. All that landscape, sand, salt-bush, with broken beer-bottle fragments along the line as a twinkling commentary on the human passage . . . . Against that vastness there are our own impositions. Travelling elsewhere inland, one can't help but notice how we've changed the face of the land, adding to and subtracting from, the original wild-life, creatures we have designed, for the ends of our industry, often without respecting them as creatures at all. In this sense, the cattle reared for food lose too often their individual uniqueness, just as we lose our own, often, in the process. I think we lose much of ourselves when we lose our sense of the world not being there merely for *us* . . .'

BRETT DIONYSIUS directed the Queensland Poetry Festival from 1997–2001 and is currently editor of *papertiger: new world poetry #05*. In 1998 he was awarded the Harri Jones Memorial Prize for Poetry by the University of Newcastle. He has co-authored one artists' book, *The Barflies' Chorus* (Lyre Bird Press, 1995) and two solo collections of poetry, *Fatherlands* (Five Islands Press, 2000) and *Bacchanalia*

(Interactive Press, 2002). *Fatherlands* was shortlisted in the 2002 Mary Gilmore Poetry Prize. He lives in Brisbane; email: brdionysius@bigpond.com.

Dionysius writes: 'The idea for "The Extinction Sonnets" came from two sources primarily. In 2003, I visited the Melbourne Museum, which had a travelling exhibition of paintings on extinct animals from around the world. Each painting had a little narrative written up beside it, extrapolating on the "end" of that particular species, and that stirred my imagination to write in the voices of these dead (Paradise Parrot) and endangered (Giant Galapagos Tortoise) animals. Secondly, the late Australian poet, Martin Johnston, was going to write a cycle of contemporary sonnets on dead and or imaginary races ("Scythians Who Want to be Scythians" etc) and so this idea of giving voice to the dispossessed (naturally and historically) grew from Johnston's original poetic vision combined with this catalytic and catastrophic exhibition of paintings. *Harriet* was picked up by Charles Darwin in 1835 and moved to Australia in 1842. She celebrates her 175th birthday this year, weighs in at 150kg and still lives at Australia Zoo with Steve Irwin.'

ALISON EASTLEY lives with her two "gorgeous, funny, intelligent and amazing" sons; their elder brother is living away, studying to be an artist. In Australia, Eastley has published work in *Island*, *Southerly*, *Meanjin*, *Four W* and the anthology *Fingers & Tongues* published by Paroxysm Press and Salt-lick Quarterly. In the USA, she has published poems in *Snow Monkey*, *The Kitchen Sink*, *Ink Pot*, the anthology *In Our Own Words*, as well as many others.

Eastley writes: '"Pipe Dreams" is a result of daydreaming about Morocco after correspondence with a friend about his experiences there. It was a wonder, a curiosity as to what I would do, how I would react if I found myself in what I feel is an exotic and enticing country.'

STEPHEN EDGAR was born in Sydney and has lived in Hobart since 1974. He is the author of five volumes of poetry, the most recent of which, *Lost in the Foreground* (Duffy&Snellgrove), won the Grace Leven Prize for Poetry and the William Baylebridge Memorial Prize for 2004. He is the winner of the inaugural *ABR* (*Australian Book Review*) Prize for poetry in 2005 for his poem "Man on the Moon." His sixth collection, *Other Summers*, is forthcoming from Black Pepper Press in 2006.

Edgar writes: 'The three poems which comprise "Pictures of Love" were originally intended to be a look at pornography. In the event only Part Two is about that subject and its dehumanizing treatment of sex. Parts One and Three deal with "real" lovers: Part One explores the idea that, even in the intimate act of love, two people remain separate worlds to each other; and Part Three treats the contrasting notion that two lovers form a world unto themselves, cut off from the world outside.'

CHRIS EDWARDS is the Sydney-based author of *Utensils in a Landscape* (Vagabond) and *A Fluke: A Mistranslation of Stéphane Mallarmé's 'Un Coup de dés'* (Monogene).

Edwards writes: 'In "Verily" I say unto you I know not what. That's the trouble with writing, said Plato, who wrote about it in *Phaedrus*. What, for example, will people make of the "huluppu-tree" in this poem? Mentioned in the *Epic of Gilgamesh*, Tablet XII, and elsewhere, it was a World Tree, possibly a willow, that belonged to Inanna, the Queen of

Heaven. Inanna was immortalised in an "Exaltation" by the priestess Enheduanna, the first author of a written work whose name we know. But some readers won't be aware of all this. Perhaps the huluppu-tree will remind them of a holiday they once had in Honolulu or Peru and how lucky they are to live in a place where the signs all point somewhere, for in this world you can't be certain. If so, they are doubly lucky. This is "the principle of identity" at work. At play it's "the idea of deciding."'

DIANE FAHEY's collections of poetry are *Voices from the Honeycomb*, *Metamorphoses*, *Turning the Hourglass*, *Mayflies in Amber*, *The Body in Time*, *Listening to a Far Sea*, and *The Sixth Swan*. She has published and read her poems internationally, and has received various poetry awards, and several writer's fellowships from the Australia Council. She is a Fellow of Hawthornden International Writers' Centre, Scotland, and has had residencies in Venice and Ireland. She holds a PhD in Creative Writing. Her views on poetry are set out in an online interview in *Thylazine*, issue 9.

About 'Fall' Fahey writes: 'Clearing ivy from around a hibiscus tree, I fell on to the stone path and did myself some damage. Laid up for six weeks, I felt at times an illusory suspension from life, but it was also a chance to recover from exhaustion and take stock. The war in Iraq was on: its great tide of deaths was in my mind when I wrote line nine. What to do with the sorrow, anger, and powerlessness one feels, now as then? I cannot get beyond this: telling the truth about the situation, and praying for hope and healing. In the small world of my poem, an enforced disengagement allows the body to heal itself, fresh energies to arise. There is, I believe, a bedrock of biological hope in us, as well as our capacity for consciously chosen or spiritually inspired hope.'

MICHAEL FARRELL is a postgraduate student at Deakin in Melbourne. *ode ode* (Salt) was published in 2003. He gives the odd writing workshop.

About 'Poem Without Dice' Farrell writes: 'I have used dice a lot in writing poems: for determining word count, line break etc. Going through Warsaw customs I emptied my pockets and forgot to retrieve the contents, which included dice. I wrote the poem during the flight to London . . . though it bears similarity to the blockier poems in *ode ode* it has a much more relaxed line. The theme's pretty relaxed too.'

PETER GOLDSWORTHY's most recent book is *This Goes With That: Collected Stories* (Viking, 2004). His *New Selected Poems* was published in Australia by Duffy&Snellgrove in 2001, and in the UK by Leviathan in 2002.

About 'Australia' Goldsworthy writes: 'This poem assembled itself during a trip to the Mildura Writers Festival, where food and poetry – and a large river – all converge each year in a wonderful turbulence. I was thinking also of those shots of earth from way, way out, a middling-sized planet floating in the void like a glistening sapphire etc – but perhaps looking less hard and gem-like than wet and delicious and very edible.'

PHILIP HAMMIAL has published eighteen collections of poetry. His sixteenth collection, *In the Year of Our Lord Slaughter's Children*, was shortlisted for the NSW Premier's Kenneth Slessor Prize in 2004, as was his fourteenth, *Bread*, in 2001. He has represented Australian at four overseas poetry festivals, most recently at the International Festival de la Poesia at Trois-Rivieres, Quebec. He is also a sculptor and the director of The Australian Collection of Outsider Art.

Hammial writes: 'As is the case with many of my poems, "Porridge" is based on a real incident. In 1963 my first wife and I did in fact get a ride hitchhiking with three Armenian gangsters (driver, boss and silent hard guy) from northern Greece into Istanbul. As they were carrying contraband, at the Turkish frontier they gave the customs officer a bottle of whiskey (the Whiskey Show). On the outskirts of the city we stopped at a restaurant where they bought us dinner and a box of baklava (the porridge) and then took us to a hotel near the Blue Mosque. The driver bargained for our room and helped us with our rucksacks. It was a great hotel, with a view from our balcony of the Bosporus, the Topkapi Palace, the Blue Mosque, etc. There weren't any nuns next door, but our neighbours on both sides seemed strange, were probably stoned, probably on opium.'

JENNIFER HARRISON is a Melbourne poet and child psychiatrist. She has written three poetry collections: *michelangelo's prisoners, Cabramatta/Cudmirrah* and *Dear B*. On behalf of the Fellowship of Australian Writers (Vic Inc.), she co-edited the 2003 Melbourne anthology *Said The Rat!* In 2003 she won the NSW Women Writers National Poetry Prize and in 2004 she was awarded the Martha Richardson Poetry Medal. Written with the support of a literary grant from the Australia Council, her new book of poems *Folly & Grief* is forthcoming from Melbourne's Black Pepper Press.

About 'The Lovely Utterly Cold Snow' Harrison writes: 'Many writers have made a simile of the blank page and snow (Yves Bonnefoy comes to mind); but here I was interested in the more clinical aspects of the writing business. Because of the strong focus on political writing at the 2003 Melbourne Writers' Festival, the contrast between the Malthouses's squashy literary buzz and the stories of tragedy in Africa and elsewhere was hard to escape – and rather melancholic. I had been especially moved by Gil Courtemanche's talk on the writing of his book, *A Sunday at the Pool in Kigali*. The PEN chair left empty each session to symbolise an author incarcerated, abused or exiled somewhere in the world follows a traditional family therapy technique of emphasising the importance of the absent one. In some ways, in such a milieu of ego and book business, the gesture struck me as self-conscious although the politic is, of course, laudable.'

KEITH HARRISON's poems have appeared widely in Australia, England and America. He has published a dozen books of poetry of which the best known are *The Complete Basho Poems* and *Changes: New & Collected Poems, 1962–2002*, which was published in America and Australia in 2003. His verse translation of *Sir Gawain and the Green Knight*, originally commissioned by the Folio Society, was subsequently chosen by Oxford University Press for their World's Classics Series (1998). He is presently working on an experimental memoir called *Not Quite Ithaka,* and the libretti for three musicals for children.

About 'An Old Woman Sings In Her Bed But Makes No Sound' Harrison writes: 'A friend, reacting angrily to a poem I wrote about an old man falling in love with a much younger woman protested "How would you react if I wrote about an old woman falling in love with a much younger man?" I thought that was, so to speak, a Germaine question as she has written much on that topic, and I urged by friend to have at it. She didn't. So, prompted by a line from a recent biography of Shackleton, I plunged in myself and produced what turned out to be a kind of stretched villanelle. The line from the

Shackleton book came from one of the sailors stranded on Elephant Island for months. Hearing that Shackleton's boat was approaching but was still some distance away, he wrote in his diary: "We are so full o joy we cannot sleep."'

J.S. HARRY lives in Sydney and has published seven poetry collections. The first, *The Deer Under the Skin* (UQP, 1971), was awarded the Harri Jones Memorial Prize. Her *New and Selected Poems* (Penguin, 1995) was shortlisted for the Victorian Premier's Prize and joint-winner of the NSW Premier's Kenneth Slessor Prize. She was a recipient of the FAW Christopher Brennan Award in 2000. Her sixth collection, *Sun Shadow, Moon Shadow* (Vagabond Press), was shortlisted for the NSW Premier's Kenneth Slessor Prize in 2001. In 2004 she edited the Youngstreet Poets' anthology, *Dreaming the Great Wave*. Her poetry has been translated into Italian, Spanish, Arabic, Polish, Slovenian and most recently, German, in the anthology *Hochzeit der Elemente* (Dumont, 2004), which includes three Peter Henry Lepus poems.

Harry writes: 'Peter Henry who appears in "Journeys West of 'War'" (parts 1 and 2) has had various other experiences in poems and books and is featured in *Sun Shadow, Moon Shadow*. He's a traveller, "a 'British' rabbit, though of Creole ancestry"; in previous poems he's had encounters with philosophers, including Bertrand Russell and Wittgenstein. I'm working on a collection for Giramondo that will include most of the Peter Henry poems previously published in book form, plus a large section of new ones, many of which, like the one here, will have Peter Henry Lepus travelling in "Iraq" in "2003." They might perhaps be read as forming a discontinuous narrative. Three of the poems which precede/lead into the "Journeys West of 'War'" included in this anthology are available on www.australia.poetryinternational.org, edited by Michael Brennan, and were first published in *Southerly*.'

KIRWAN HENRY lives and teaches a junior primary class in Blackstone, a remote Aboriginal community in the West Australian desert.

About 'Bee Season' Henry writes: 'This poem was written a couple of summers ago. I'd had a dream in which I was stung by bees. I wrote with the image of the bees and the pain of their stings still fresh in my mind.'

GRAEME HETHERINGTON is a Tasmanian Poet who divides his time between Australia and Europe.

About 'Athenian Wolves' Hetherington writes: 'I still remember the shock of recognition when I saw the lone wolf in its fenced enclosure in the Zappeion Gardens in Athens. Its situation and appearance forcibly reminded me of my own at the time and set the poem in motion. This was in 1986, but I didn't lick it into sufficiently good shape to submit for publication until last year. Then it was only because Les Murray at *Quadrant* suggested the inversion of two words in the the concluding stages of the poem that I was able to get it exactly right. Indeed, such is the nature of the poem that it is perhaps understandable that I was hesitant in exploring this encounter with the Zappeion wolf to its poetical resolution.'

RICHARD HILLMAN lives in South Australia with his wife and three children. He completed a PhD on the Australian poet Francis Webb in 2004. His fourth and most recent collection of poetry is *Jabiluka Honey: New & Selected Poems* (Bookends

Books, 2003). He has been published widely in Australia, New Zealand, Canada, USA, China, Europe and the United Kingdom. Former poetry editor of *SideWaLK* and *Thylazine*, he is currently a contributing editor for *papertiger*.

Hillman writes: '"The Big Wet Takes Hold" followed an enthusiastic conversation with the artist, writer and editor John von Sturmer, after he mentioned correspondence in the *Springfield Gazette* about the "big wet taking hold" in Warburton (WA). I thought this truly Indigenous statement had larger metaphorical implications than a simple reference to the beginning of the wet season. This text concerns the comedy of human activity and its repetition, as part of seasonal cycles, in Australian society. As if to confirm what I have written, there has been a running of the brides and a running of the shoppers since the poem was accepted for publication in *Meanjin*. From what JvS has said, I gather that *"toujours les poubelles"* (always the garbage) is a statement stated by landlords in Paris, apparently to justify the raising of the rent – although I've interpreted the statement ironically as "goodbye to the pong", I feel as if it means "the garbage goes". From memory, South Australian state parliamentarians were considering the cost of dealing with waste from the Olympic Dam uranium mine when I wrote the poem two years ago.'

CLIVE JAMES's most recent of many books are his collected poems, *The Book of My Enemy*, and a book of essays, *Even As We Speak*. A new book of essays, *The Meaning of Recognition*, will be published later this year. He is currently working on a fourth volume of his unreliable memoirs, and on developing his multimedia personal website, www.clivejames.com. In 2003 he was awarded the Philip Hodgins Memorial Medal and is a member of the Order of Australia.

About 'William Dobell's Cypriot' James writes: 'Whenever I visited the Art Gallery of Queensland in Brisbane, William Dobell's portrait of The Cypriot bowled me over, and finally I found myself writing a poem about it. Almost every assumption I made about Dobell's inspiration for the painting turned out to be wrong. He met and first drew the Cypriot in London, for example, and not in Australia. But the poem's story about the influence of the European immigrants on post-war Australian culture is the truest story I know, so I am happy that the poem managed to attain an independent life before I could get hold of it and scrap it.'

JOHN JENKINS lives in Kangaroo Ground, on the rural fringe of Melbourne. He is a poet, journalist, editor, teacher and reviewer. His most recent non-fiction title is *Travelers' Tales of Old Cuba* (Ocean Press, 2002) and poetry books are *Dark River* (Five Islands Press, 2003) and the verse novel *A Break in the Weather* (Modern Writing Press, 2003).

Of 'Under the Shaded Blossom' Jenkins writes: 'This poem has been very good to me, and seems to have "legs." As winner of the 2004 James Joyce Foundation Suspended Sentence Award, it took me on a six-week trip to Ireland, Paris and Beijing. It was published in *Heat* and now *The Best Australian Poetry 2005*. Finally, a dramatised version, complete with audio treatment, will go to air in ABC Radio National's *Airplay* series. The poem records an unlikely meeting in Havana, and a wary battle of wits between two "odd fish." Meyer Lansky's shady dealings and dirty doings in Havana have been well documented by the Cuban writer Enrique Cirules, while the great American poet Wallace Stevens first visited Havana in 1923. Whether he made subsequent visits is unclear, though he often skipped down to Florida and Miami.

Although their meeting is highly moot, sinister slickers like Lansky often rubbed shoulders – in the casinos of bad old Havana – with respectable businessmen such as Stevens. For those who like literary clues: fragments and echoes of several famous poems by Wallace Stevens here become part of the poet's daydreams and musings, roused by the slightly delirious atmosphere of Havana. In his letters, Stevens writes that Cuba reminded him of certain brine-scented scenes in *The Tempest*, and echoes of Shakespeare's play also sometimes shade into Stevens' interior monologues. The poet's letters reveal much about the man, as do his philosophical reflections on the poetic imagination, some fragments of which I also quote. "Big Lucky" refers to Lucky Luciano, Lansky's boss and head of the Sicilian Mafia in New York. Finally, though my two characters are based on real people, they are purely fictional – as is their imaginary meeting.'

EVAN JONES, born in 1931, has published four books of poems: *Inside the Whale* (Cheshire, 1960), *Understandings* (Cambridge UP, 1967), *Recognitions* (ANUP, 1978) and *Left at the Post* (UQP, 1984).

About 'Buddha and the Society of Jesus' Jones writes: 'I visited Sri Lanka in February 2003, and my daughter and I did indeed meet a man called Anuradha, who was a guide at Anuradhapura and told my daughter that he must have been fated to be a guide there because of his name. He talked about religious architecture and the way in which temples, churches, *stupas*, etc all fulfil a similar geometric pattern. We talked about religion a little and I remarked that many people in Sri Lanka seem to be Jesuit educated. Thus the poem in its entirety is straightforwardly true.'

AILEEN KELLY grew up in England and is now an adult educator in Melbourne. Her first book, *Coming up for Light*, won the Mary Gilmore Award and the Vincent Buckley Prize, and was shortlisted for the Victorian Premier's Poetry Award. Her work is widely published in Australia, Ireland and elsewhere. Her most recent collection of poems is *City and Stranger* (Five Islands Press, 2002).

About 'His Visitors' Kelly writes: 'It started as one of those proto-poems that emerge from the subconscious in the middle of the night, in the form of some visual images, a mood and a few phrases. I can guess, as one does with a dream, what news stories might have encouraged it – about survivalist, conspiracy-theorist, anti-authority groups engaged in military training in the hills outside several major cities; and the "graduation" of some gang-associated youths into apparently conventional citizens who continue to be involved in counter-culture. I hadn't set out to write a poem about this, but when it suggested itself I liked its potential for being a disturbing experience, a sense of menace set off-key in a pleasant semi-rural residential area.'

JOHN KINSELLA's most recent volumes of poetry are *Doppler Effect: Collected Experimental Poems* (Salt, 2004) and *The New Arcadia* (FACP, 2005). He is Professor of English at Kenyon College, Ohio; Fellow of Churchill College, Cambridge University; and a Principal of the Landscape and Language Centre at Edith Cowan University, Western Australia. He has recently founded the International School of Environmental Poetics and Creativity.

Kinsella writes: '"The Vital Waters" was formulated over many years of living in Cambridge, England. What struck me from the moment I arrived there was how the university – so loud in its environment – was only one part of that town. A university town, to be sure, but also one in which whole lives barely come into contact with its day-to-day workings. One can't help but be affected by its buildings and public rituals, but the old "town and gown" divide is alive and well. And within the university there are many divides, many spaces people don't cross into. The great Cantabrigian (though he has and had nothing directly to do with the university), to me, has always been Syd Barrett, the musician, apostate member of early Pink Floyd, whimsical lyricist of brilliance, who experienced a dramatic fall from "sanity" and the public eye. I have been writing a Syd Barrett poem for twenty-five years. That he lives an anonymous and hermetic life entirely disconnected from his fame, becomes metaphor for the way Cambridge cloaks its inhabitants. Someone once said to me in College: you don't need to leave this island in the fens; eventually, the world comes to you. The problems with this inward-lookingness are obvious, but there's no doubt the ancient stone of Cambridge is a conduit for many cross-pollinating conversations, not the least from Australia.'

ZOLTAN KOVACS is a Hungarian-born Australian poet. He and his family came to Australia in 1972 from communist Hungary. He fell in love with the English language while learning it (Magyar having been his mother tongue before arrival in Australia). He is forty years of age and has been writing poetry for at least twenty-seven of those. Along with a recent volume of poetry called *Haymaking,* he has been published in various magazines and newspapers in Australia, the US and England.

Kovacs writes: '"Ghosts" is based on a real archaeological find in the Severn Estuary. The premise of the poem is that there is no such thing as "modern" and "civilisation," there is only such a thing as life. It is only a conceit of succeeding generations that they are the apotheosis of life on earth, and that people who walked barefoot and gathered cockles and mussels on the seashore were somehow "primitive." The poem is also meant to echo the simple pleasure that these people must have taken in gathering their food on what may have been a beautiful day. The last line is an admonition to our time; perhaps if we retuned to simpler lives we might rediscover optimism. If we understood this planet is our only planet, as a species we could relearn the art of gentleness, playfulness and concern.'

ANTHONY LAWRENCE's most recent book of poems is *The Sleep of a Learning Man*, which was shortlisted for the Victorian Premier's Prize.

Lawrence writes: '"Wandering Albatross" began at sea, off the Tasman Peninsula, in the Great Southern Ocean. I didn't have pen or paper on board, so the first ten lines were "written" on the back of an aluminium lure-tray, scratched in by a screwdriver. For those fishing out on the Continental Shelf, Wandering and other species of albatross are not uncommon, and their wingspan, when seen at close range, is truly amazing. The poem began and ended as a kind of travelogue, which includes distribution and windy demographic. For me to write a land or sea-based poem with no reference to or connection with humans is unusual. Here, pure description demanded my attention.'

GEOFFREY LEHMANN is married to Gail Pearson and has five children and one grandchild. He works as a tax lawyer with an international accounting firm. His best-known book of verse *Spring Forest* was published by Faber & Faber in 1994 and was shortlisted for the T.S. Eliot Prize. He is still adding poems to this sequence. His *Collected Poems* was published by Heinemann Australia in 1997.

About 'Thirteen Long-Playing Haiku' Lehmann writes: 'This is an autobiographical poem which is about obsession. The poem is strictly factual, with two small exceptions. In the opening piece, I have imagined the amateur broadcaster, my ghostly alter ego, washing his LPs – I have no idea whether he did this. Also in the coda at the end, I have assembled an "ideal" selection of CDs to play in my car as I drive through the night.'

KATHRYN LOMER has a background in teaching ESL. Her book of poetry, *Extraction of Arrows*, won the 2003 National FAW Anne Elder Award for a first collection. Her other books are a novel, *The god in the ink*, and a novel for young adults, *The Spare Room*. All are published by UQP.

About 'Tibetan Windhorse' Lomer writes: 'This poem was written when the seasonal changes in my immediate environment impacted on, and reflected, my emotional state. It was a time of uncertainty and ambiguity. A *koi-nobori* kite flew in my garden. (*Koi-nobori* is Japanese for the carp, which swims upriver.) The kite reminded me of the windhorse, used by Tibetans to determine the direction of their travels. I had always loved the image (and the name!). I decided to borrow the idea for some private meaning-making.'

JENNIFER MAIDEN was born in Penrith, NSW on 7 April 1949. Thirteen of her poetry collections (one including short stories) and two of her novels have been published. She has won the NSW Premier's Prize twice, the Victorian Premier's Prize, the Christopher Brennan Award for a lifetime of achievement in poetry, and many other awards. She has been Writer in Residence at the Australian National University, University of Western Sydney, Springwood High School and the NSW Torture and Trauma Rehabilitation Service. Her novel *Play With Knives* has been translated and published by dtv in Germany. Her next collection, *Friendly Fire*, is forthcoming from Giramondo.

About 'Thunderbolt's Way' Maiden writes: 'On many levels, interpretation of this poem is as usual open to the reader. Technically, however, "Thunderbolt's Way" is related but has a different structure to those pieces I call my "cluster poems", in which disparate subjects and metaphors run parallel and then tie in together. In it, for me, the two themes of the erosion of literature by situational conservatism, and the loss and re-assertion of humanity in historical speculation ride side by side but are tied in at the end by a question meant to echo both plights through specific personality (all the personalities here seemed to me to have been very poignant). In the course of the writing, I was not just striving for a Koestler-like creative marriage of unlikely elements but also for an illumination by parallel flow and final solitary but synthesising emotional tone.'

LES MURRAY's poems from the first 40-odd years of his career are gathered in his *Collected Poems 1961–2002* (Duffy & Snellgrove, 2002). His other books include *Fredy Neptune* (verse novel, 1998); *A Working Forest* (selected prose, 1997); and *The Full Dress* (poems matched with works in The National Gallery of Australia, 2001). He has won major prizes in Australia, Britain, and Germany, and his work has been published in seven European languages; further translations, into Hindi and Italian, are in progress.

About 'Travelling the British Roads' Murray writes: 'While

a native of Bunyah, I am also an old Welsh driver, having learned to drive on the serpentine roads of Glamorgan in 1967. In most years since, I have returned to Britain for further short bouts of time-travel.'

Joyce Parkes has published poetry in privileged, in progressive and in innovative literary magazines, newspapers, e-zines – in print, and on-line – in Australia, England, Finland, Canada, Germany, the USA. One of her peace poems can be viewed on www.thylazine.org. More of her peace poems can be read in the *New England Review* and in *Word-Thirst*.

Parkes writes: '"Propinquity's Premise" began at an Adelaide's Writers' Festival, was nurtured at one of Sydney's Writers' Weeks and at a Cusco, Peru, Cultural Festival, where chequered moments and "Thank you for the life" became part of the poem, to sojourn to Vancouver B.C., Toronto, New York, New York, and London, England, where Yvonne Best, my host, displayed ogive-veined hands. Her daughter Charity Haynes – my staunchest and finest friend – found the image too obscure to further the poem. How to articulate our similarities. Adieux and accents, naturally. "Propinquity's Premise" then travelled to Manchester, Belfast, Port Stewart, Port Rush, Sligo and Drumcliff. Returning to Sligo Train Station, the first title came to mind: Festival Stations. The poem was further worked for, written towards, in Darlington, Western Australia, and later in Ballajura on the Swan coastal plains, from where "Propinquity's Premise" was submitted to John Leonard, Poetry Editor at *Overland*.'

Dorothy Porter has published six collections of poetry and four verse novels. Her most recent publication is the chapbook

Poems: January–August 2004 (Vagabond Press, 2004). Her last verse novel *Wild Surmise* won both the Poetry and Premier's prizes at the Adelaide Festival Awards 2004.

About 'Ode To Agatha Christie' Porter writes: 'Like many poets I am an addicted reader of crime fiction. And many crime writers have been great readers of poetry. What is the link? Perhaps in both there is an urge to cut to the chase and an underlying or even overt obsession with death. I regard Agatha Christie as one of my dearest friends, to whom I turn when I'm going through a dark and troubled time. She's the best possible company in illness. I have been reading her with delight and relish since I was twelve and I felt an ode in her honour was long overdue. I decided to write it in reasonably regular rhyming stanzas – as a show of respect.'

PHILOMENA VAN RIJSWIJK's first collection of poems, *Trail of Bones and Godstones*, and her first novel, *The Time It Rained Fish*, were published by Esperance Press, Tasmania. Her second novel, *The World as a Clockface*, was published by Penguin in 2001. Her poems can be found in many literary journals and anthologies. She was co-editor of *Coastlines,* an Indonesian/Australian literary magazine. During 2003 she was writer-in-residence at both Risdon men's and women's prisons in southern Tasmania. Her work was included in *Best Australian Stories 2002* (Black Inc) and is being translated into Hindi by Dr Aruna Sitesh.

Rijswijk writes: '"My Beautiful Whitewashed Skin" was inspired by an episode of *Global Village*. The segment was about a town somewhere in Eastern Europe, where the women whitewash and repaint their houses and fences each year, decorating them with colourful motifs, mostly of garlands of flowers. The sense of ritual and renewal reminded me of the processes that I had been going through, having found myself single for the first time since the age of eighteen. Contrary to popular mythology, celibacy and singledom can be a celebration; aloneness can be exquisite. I wanted to make the sense of separateness in this poem delicious and wholesome, like the feel of fresh, cold sheets and clean feet.'

PETER ROSE is currently the editor of *Australian Book Review*. His most recent collection is *Rattus Rattus: New and Selected Poems* (2005). Other publications include *Rose Boys*, which won the 2003 National Biography Award, and a novel, *A Case of Knives* (2005).

About 'Quotidian' Rose writes: 'This may be a heresy, but much poetry is a kind of twisting autobiography, subject to constant revision. My poem "Quotidian" pecks away at the past, extracting incidents and recollections, even particular tastes and sounds. The associations are free, if elegiac. Bernstein is the "febrile conductor."'

CRAIG SHERBORNE is a poet, playwright and journalist. His 1995 poetry collection, *Bullion*, was published by Penguin. He won the Wal Cherry Play of the Year for his La Mama (Melbourne) produced drama, *The Ones of Town*. His 1999 verse-drama *Look at Everything Twice for Me* was on the VCE syllabus for two years. He works as a reporter at the *Herald Sun* in Melbourne. His memoir, *Hoi Polloi*, the first instalment of a trilogy, will be published by Black Inc in September 2005. Black Inc will also bring out his new collection of poetry early in 2006.

About 'Journo' Sherborne writes: 'I spend my weekdays working as a reporter on a major daily newspaper. It has often occurred to me that such work involves cheerily exploiting the misfortunes and misdeeds of people I've never met, for processing into an attention-seeking story that assures my wages are paid. No matter how any reporter tries to be responsible in the course of that work, and asserts that it is done in the public interest, we become desensitised to other people's suffering. Indeed suffering and human folly become commodities used for good copy and little more.'

PETER STEELE, a Jesuit priest, has taught for many years at the University of Melbourne. His most recent book is *Plenty: Art into Poetry* (Macmillan Australia, 2003).

About 'Vermeer's Geographer' Steele writes: 'I have written many poems about works of art, and it is hard to go past Vermeer. I am greatly taken, in his "Geographer," by the combination of quest and estimation, a combination which may inform my own work whether in poetry or in prose. Perhaps poetry is itself a "geographer of the imagination" though, if so, my poem bears on a small island, while Vermeer is about oceans and continents.'

HUGH TOLHURST born in Melbourne in 1966. Through an Australia Council for the Arts Skills and Arts Development Grant, he spent six months at the BR Whiting Library in Rome, during which time in Italy he was also a guest of *Napoli Poesia*. Black Pepper published *Filth and Other Poems* in 1997 and he has a second collection forthcoming. He also reviews poetry for various newspapers and journals and is a poetry reader for Black Pepper.

About 'Some Music in the Chiesa San Carlino' Tolhurst writes: 'You never meet anyone from Rome in Rome, even

Francesco Borromini (1599–1667) was from Lombardy, though I guess he might have got to meet a Roman or two. Living there is a terrific experience, and affording artists the chance to apply for international studios is one of the strongest programs of the Australia Council. New poets have so few book publishing opportunities; I'm of the view that the first collections publishers are currently rejecting are sometimes stronger in literary merit than the published first collections of a year like, say, 1968.'

JOHN TRANTER has published twenty collections of verse, including *Heart Print, Studio Moon* and *Trio* (all published by Salt in the UK). In 1992 he edited (with Philip Mead) the *Penguin Book of Modern Australian Poetry,* which has become the standard text in its field. He has lived at various times in Melbourne, Singapore, Brisbane, London, and other places, and now lives in Sydney, where he is a company director. He is the editor of the free Internet magazine *Jacket*, at www.jacketmagazine.com. The University of Queensland Press will publish his *New and Selected Poems* in 2006.

About 'Transatlantic' Tranter writes: 'I have always felt that the work of the hoax poet Ern Malley (1918–43) is more lively and interesting than most other Australian poetry. I was born the year he died, and I feel there may have been a touch of metempsychosis at work and a concomitant obligation to carry the baton of experimental writing into the next century. Recently I wrote a series of ten poems in or through the "voice" of Ern Malley, speaking in turn through the voices of other writers, in a kind of double ventriloquy. In "Transatlantic" Ern speaks through the monotone of Gertrude Stein as it is heard in her *The Autobiography of Alice B. Toklas*.'

CHRIS WALLACE-CRABBE is a poet, essayist and former Director of The Australian Centre at Melbourne University. His latest book is a long poem, *The Universe Looks Down* (Brandl & Schlesinger); while a critical volume, *Read It Again*, is shortly due from Salt Publishing.

About 'From the Island, Bundanon' Wallace-Crabbe writes: 'Two years ago my partner and I took up a joint residency at Bundanon, Arthur Boyd's old property on the lower Shoalhaven River. Both of us responded impressionistically to this marvellous site, but how were all these sensations to be translated? In my case a focus had to be found, along with a sprawling enough poetic form. I focused on Bundanon's wild, stony island in the river, which was so various as to capture Bundanon in pathless miniature, and on this reflective suite. Thomas Hardy thought landscape was all washed up, but it isn't, yet.'

FAY ZWICKY, born in 1933, is a poet, short story author and essayist. Her most recent collection of poetry, *The Gatekeeper's Wife*, was published by Brandl & Schlesinger in 1997.

About 'Makassar, 1956' Zwicky writes: 'Never believe writers who pretend that they don't base their work on their own experience: the presences of people and places this poet has known are inescapable. Now as grandmother, chastened and nourished by rich floods of memory, I write against the coming dark.'

SERIES EDITORS' BIOGRAPHIES

BRONWYN LEA was born in Tasmania in 1969, grew up in Queensland and Papua New Guinea, and lived in Califonia for twelve years. She is the author of *Flight Animals* (UQP, 2001), which won the Wesley Michel Wright Prize for Poetry and FAW Anne Elder Poetry Award. She lectures in Poetics and Narrative at the University of Queensland.

MARTIN DUWELL was born in England and has lived in Australia since 1957. He was a publisher of contemporary Australian poetry in the seventies and eighties and since that time has written widely on the subject in essays and reviews. He is the author of a set of interviews with poets, *A Possible Contemporary Poetry* (Makar, 1982) and, with R.M.W. Dixon, is the editor of two anthologies of Aboriginal song poetry: *The Honey-Ant Men's Love Song* (UQP, 1990) and *Little Eva at Moonlight Creek* (UQP, 1994). He has also edited an edition of the *Selected Poems of John Blight* and was one of the editors of the *Penguin New Literary History of Australia* (Penguin, 1988). He has strong interest in medieval Icelandic literature and Persian language and literature.

Journals Where the Poems First Appeared

The Age, poetry ed. Gig Ryan. 250 Spencer Street, Melbourne, VIC 3000.

The Australian, ed. Barry Hill. GPO Box 4245, Sydney, NSW 2001.

The Australian Book Review, ed. Peter Rose. PO Box 2320, Richmond South, VIC 3121.

Blue Dog: Australian Poetry, ed. Ron Pretty. c/o Poetry Australia. PO Box U34, Wollongong University, NSW 2500.

Boxkite: A Journal of Poetry and Poetics, ed. James Taylor. PO Box 161, Pyrmont, NSW 2009.

Eureka Street, poetry ed. Philip Harvey. PO Box 553, Richmond, VIC 3121.

Famous Reporter, ed. Ralph Wessman. PO Box 368, North Hobart, TAS 7002.

Heat, poetry ed. Lucy Dougan. Dean's Unit, CAESS, University of Western Sydney, Locked Bag 1797, Penrith South DC, NSW 1797.

Hecate: An Interdisplinary Journal of Women's Liberation, ed. Carole Ferrier. PO Box 6099 St Lucia, QLD 4067.

Island, ed. Peter Owen. PO Box 210, Sandy Bay, TAS 7006.

Meanjin, poetry ed. Judith Beveridge. 131 Barry Street, Carlton, VIC 3053.

Overland, poetry ed. John Leonard. VU-Footscray Park, PO Box 14428, Melbourne, VIC 8001.

Quadrant, poetry ed. Les Murray. PO Box 82, Balmain, NSW 2041.

Southerly, ed. David Brooks. Department of English, Woolley Building A20, University of Sydney, NSW 2006.

ACKNOWLEDGMENTS

The general editors would like to thank Carol Hetherington for her research assistance with this book. Grateful acknowledgment is made to the following publications from which the poems in this volume were chosen:

Bruce Beaver, 'A Schizoid Poem.' *Southerly* 63.2 (2003): 26–27.

Judith Beveridge, 'The Shark.' *Heat* 8 NS (2004): 163.

Javant Biarujia, 'Icarus.' *Heat* 8 NS (2004): 107.

MTC Cronin, 'The Dust in Everything.' *Meanjin* 63.4 (2004): 26–27.

Bruce Dawe, 'Othernesses Other Than Our Own.' *Southerly* 63.2 (2003): 149.

Brett Dionysius, '*from* The Extinction Sonnets.' *Meanjin* 63.1 (2004): 234.

Alison Eastley, 'Pipe Dreams.' *Salt-lick: New Poetry* 4 (2004): 16.

Stephen Edgar, 'Pictures of Love.' *Island* 97 (2004): 50–53.

Chris Edwards, 'Verily.' *Boxkite* 3/4 (2004): 131.

Diane Fahey, 'Fall.' Blue *Dog: Australian Poetry* 3.6 (2004): 31.

Michael Farrell, 'poem without dice.' *Eureka Street* (April, 2004): 15.

Peter Goldsworthy, 'Australia.' *Quadrant* 48.7–8 (Jul–Aug, 2004): 45.

Philip Hammial, 'Porridge.' *Blue Dog: Australian Poetry* 3.6 (2004): 43.

Jennifer Harrison, 'The Lovely Utterly Cold Snow.' *Salt-lick: New Poetry* 4 (2004): 61.

Keith Harrison, 'The Old Woman Sings in Her Bed but Makes no Sound.' *Australian Book Review* 263 (Aug, 2004): 8.

J.S. Harry, 'Journeys West of "War."' *Heat* 7 NS (2004): 58–70.

Graeme Hetherington, 'Athenian Wolves.' *Quadrant* 48.6 (Jun, 2004): 85.

Kirwan Henry, 'Bee Season.' *Heat* 8 NS (2004): 141.

Richard Hillman, 'The Big Wet Takes Hold.' *Meanjin* 63.4 (2004): 216–17.

Clive James, 'William Dobell's Cypriot.' *Australian Book Review* 259 (Mar, 2004): 20.

John Jenkins, 'Under the Shaded Blossom.' *Heat* 8 NS (2004): 44–54.

Evan Jones, 'Buddha and the Society of Jesus.' *Eureka Street* (Oct , 2004): 6.

Aileen Kelly, 'His Visitors.' *The Age* 16 October, 2004 Review: 4.

John Kinsella, 'The Vital Waters.' *Meanjin* 63.3 (2004): 206–15.

Zoltan Kovacs, 'Ghosts.' *Famous Reporter* 30 (2004): 141.

Anthony Lawrence, 'Wandering Albatross.' *Australian Book Review* 262 (Jun–Jul, 2004): 33.

Geoffrey Lehmann, 'Thirteen Long-Playing Haiku.' *Heat* 7 NS (2004): 215–20.

Kathryn Lomer, 'Tibetan Windhorse.' *Southerly* 63.2 (2003): 93.

Jennifer Maiden, 'Thunderbolt's Way.' *Southerly* 63.2 (2003): 44–45.

Les Murray, 'Travelling the British Roads.' *Meanjin* 63.3 (2004): 20–22.

Joyce Parkes, 'Propinquity's Premise.' *Overland* 177 (2004): 91.

Dorothy Porter, 'Ode to Agatha Christie.' *Heat* 8 NS (2004): 165–66.

Philomena van Rijswijk, 'My Beautiful Whitewashed Skin.' *Hecate* 30.1 (2004): 106.

Peter Rose, 'Quotidian.' *Meanjin* 63.1 (2004): 2–3.

Craig Sherborne, 'Journo.' *Quadrant* 48.9 (Sept, 2004): 67.

Peter Steele, 'Vermeer's Geographer.' *The Weekend Australian* 14–15 August, 2004 Review: 15.

Hugh Tolhurst, 'Some Music in the Chiesa San Carlo.' *Quadrant* 48.1–2 (Jan–Feb, 2004): 116.

John Tranter, 'Transatlantic.' *Meanjin* 63.4 (2004): 12–13.

Chris Wallace-Crabbe, 'From the Island, Bundanon.' *Meanjin* 63.1 (2004): 172–74.

Fay Zwicky, 'Makassar, 1956.' *Heat* 8 NS (2004): 55–60.

THE JOSEPHINE ULRICK POETRY PRIZE 2006

The Josephine Ulrick and Win Schubert Foundation for the Arts
are the proud sponsors of Australia's richest prize for poetry.
It is named in memory of Josephine Ulrick
whose three great loves were art, literature and photography.

FIRST PRIZE IS $10,000
AWARDED TO A POEM OR SUITE OF POEMS UP TO
TWO HUNDRED LINES

For prize dates and conditions of entry contact:
Josephine Ulrick Poetry Prize 2006,
Attention Sonia Pucki,
School of Arts,
Gold Coast Campus Griffith University,
PMB 50, Gold Coast Mail Centre, Qld 9726, Australia

s.pucki@gu.edu.au
www.gu.edu/school/art/ulrick
ph. (07) 5552-8428

PREVIOUS WINNERS OF THE JOSEPHINE ULRICK POETRY PRIZE
2005: Chris Fontana
2004: Nathan Shepherdson
2003: Judith Beveridge
2002: Judy Johnson
2001: Anthony Lawrence
2000: Kathryn Lomer
1999: Jean Kent

The winning entry for 2005 follows.

CHRIS FONTANA

HUSBANDRY

Here's what I am
I smell of lavender. A pale smell of not quite purple, of weak
tea or diluted wine. I am a garden smell that grows out of earth
but belongs to the wind. I grow out of dung but wear myself in
the air.

Here's what I'm not
I'm not my own flowers. I get my lavender from a bottle and
splash it on skin. I don't grow flowers because flowers die and
you can't eat what you see, and you can't bite with your eye-
lids, and because nothing here is without its purpose, I grow
vegetables instead. I grow them in neat rows behind fences
that he knocks up. When he says grow 'something pretty' I
grow rose-lip crevices inside my cabbages. My vegetables fold
into themselves, like hard green vaginas.

I get my lavender from a bottle because I think he'll like me as
flowers, and I grow vegetables in rows with my fingers plung-
ing into the same dirt he walks on with hard boots. I know the
land like the back of my hands, where it catches its dust on fine
hair.

When I'm big with child I'll hang from the bedhead like a
carcass, my pink flesh prettied by pink texta words. I'll be

apportioned by broken lines into many meals, of flank for the boys and breast for the men, and he'll touch me with those hands that are spanners, hands that have rust, hands of his that knock up what nature knocks down, knocking up against me where I hang, a carcass.

What I'm not is – I'm not big with child.

Here's what he thinks
That those hands of his know the land like their backs, hands that pummel its bones with mallets, pummel strong metal skeletons that shape its fields into holding yards and pig pens. We keep our animals in rib cages. They run along femur and fibula, they brush up against humerus and radius. His fences are dead metal skeletons that clatter in the wind. He knocks up the fences and nature knocks them down. Because life is symmetry nature knocks them down and he knocks them up again. Outside our window is a map of clean lines, like veins on the back of his hand, where he knows it, this land. Hands that can turn an udder into a tap.

Here's what I think
Landscape is female and doesn't like to be fenced.

When we gather next door he smells of beer. He gets his beer from a bottle and splashes it on skin, and I toss the salad while he turns the meat, and I watch her watch him. She's our neighbour. She lives there, but might have lived here. If things had been different. And I wonder sometimes about what he did to her in the back of his car. If it's the same as what he does to me. In the bed. If pillow talk is different over vinyl armrests.

What he does now is
He stands with the boys and talks of toy soldiers. Soldiers he knew when he was young, who gave pennies to skylarking lads. And his mouth is lined with yeast. And he talks of his father's legacy of yesterday, of his grandfather's legacy of yesteryear. Of his greatgrandfather's grave out there behind the shed. And here's what they see when they gather round to hear how he has his roots in this land, how he grows out of his greatgrandfather's bones buried so far under, how he crawls under the dirt and bursts out yawning like a sapling. True, he has tree-trunk legs. And he gets louder as they get closer, the boys, and when he turns the meat they read the back of his hand like tea leaves.

What they do as they get closer is they all get louder with the words of their fathers their grandfathers their greatgrandfathers, until there are so many roots under our dirt they're all tangled. I toss salad and see that to them this land is theirs because of the way it holds death. At the table are their wives all tossing salad, her too, all big with child, her too, all preparing to give birth, to what. To more bodies to bury, under the dirt with their greatgreatgrandfathers.

In the fertile soil of my garden I never did dig up bones.

What he likes is
Ladies. Like the bull. One bull on our farm and what it likes is
ladies, though it sometimes gets confused with the castrated
calves, not really boys anymore, though they still pee through
a penis, somehow their stink not quite the same. And he talks
to the boys so that the ladies can hear him. Loud. And later in
the confusion of cooked meat, when the genders mingle to fill
their plates, he'll lean in close and touch them big belly to big
belly. They'll guess what's swelling underneath it, though they
won't guess that it's only a pipeline, to a swamp, alive with
dead tadpoles. Not even he will guess that, impressing them
with banter about how girls gabble like geese, reaching over
for tossed coleslaw, tossing off with his tongue while I turn
blind eyes with stainless steel tongs.

What he doesn't tell them is
How the cat birthed her kittens in our hamper. How he took
them too quickly, before they took suck. How he took them to
the bucket, and with the same hand that turns the meat held
them under. He tells them over dinner, though, *God the things
I have to do,* and I think of how he uses God and himself in the
same sentence.

What they don't know is
When we get home the cat will curl herself around his ankles.

Here's what I don't see. How he looks at her, big with her own
husband's child, and probably remembers what he said to her
over vinyl armrests, which is or is not different from what he
doesn't say to me.

Here's what she is

She smells of something you could eat. Something you could lick with your tongue, and that's why I lap behind my closed lips. He watches her because he likes the way she dresses in lace. Lace on top and lace underneath, we both know, because I've watched her too, in other places, in other company, where women – us – drink tea and indulge in what he calls our nothing-better-to-do.

Afraid that he'll say nothing I wear no lace, but dress myself in Jersey and Friesian. I dress myself in his everyday to become and to remain his familiar. She dresses in lace and fire and flood and smells of something you could eat. She looks at him when he tastes her fine floral lace with his eyes, she looks at him that way, and I wonder if I dressed his trousers like a rough sack over my smooth legs would she look at me like that.

When I'm big with child I'll hang from the bedhead like a carcass, smelling less like air, and he'll turn me with his hands like I was basted meat and at least be hungry.

What he does is

Before we leave he rests his hands on her belly to feel the baby kick. The eyes of her husband watch my husband but because he's not in cattle he doesn't know to be suspicious of would-be bulls, and anyhow doesn't have the wherewithal to castrate, though the taste of turps is on his tongue. My husband's balls would move inside themselves when pinched in his hands. They fit there, I know, in that warm cup, but spill no blood that isn't without its purpose.

What I know is

The eyes of her husband aren't so hungry now because when he tills the soil and his seeds are sown, his half of the work is already done. It's done before winter and in the cycle of their farm winter is a time of rest and waiting. Let there be no mistake, when he tills the soil it's with steel blades and clean hands on tractor-tops. There'll be no dirt on his knees when winter comes and the fields grow fat and heavy, no inviting soil to turn, all earthly bodies lumbering and graceless.

At home

That their bellies are lop-sided is how you tell. Round bellies with bumps, Friesian ladies with two hooves deeper in the dirt and walking-stick gaits. My husband puts his hands on cow-bellies. He smooths their flanks, so gentle, and lets them lie-in, away from the milkers. Away from the company of women when she needs them most.

His cows

They deliver in the dark, where everything goes by feel. They deliver at standstill in the dark and we follow the bellowing, our feet falling into potholes. We go by feel and by torchlight, going by gumboot, by a shift in the air, worming our way into the night like his roots through the dirt. Worming our way to her and her secret women's business. She delivers in modesty but for that one small leg – stuck – and I think Nature how could you, Nature not a woman afterall, Nature with design flaws. Nature putting a cattle grid inside her that the calf can't cross. His hand disappears up the rear-end of her – the only warm place – and I watch his face as he burrows and remembers, birthing himself a hundred times as he feels the wet stick of a leg, and he unfolds, or turns or pulls it downwards – easy Darlin' – pulls it downwards. His arm up inside her is soup stock, is flavouring the afterbirth before it falls to the earth, where she'll taste from the inside of herself – like I do – him.

He's raw flesh and turd smell over dinner. He's hands wiped on tea towels. He showers but the smell stays. In bed his hands leave rust stains on the sheets. He leaves fine rust powders. His hands are cold on my skin, but when our hides touch he is warm cow bodies and my body is ready. By then, though, he's had enough of the insides of women.

I think myself awake with thoughts of the sluice of bodies and the new calf on stick legs. Of how he thinks nothing of the cold morning act of measuring the new meat, of sizing up its sex, breeder or bred. He'll steal the babe, god child of his deliverance, male or female he'll steal the child and say over its skinny body *strong bones she'll bear young and be a good milker,* and I'll think of my slight frame too-brittle, of my small breasts and my flat belly. Or he'll say over its skinny body *good flanks poor bugger we'll fatten him up and get a good price for him,* though he won't be a him for much longer.

What he'll do is
He'll steal the babe and the mother will cry in the paddock for days, mourning while he squeezes her udders for milk, our must-have, milk for all the grown men. He'll be turning the udders into taps, mothers suckled by steel mouths they can't love. That's why he does it. Mothers' milk, that's what he's

about. All mouths at the breast of this land he knows like the back of his hand, stealing milk from the mouths of babes.

What they don't do is
They don't step inside the milking shed to see that mothers milk can smell this bad.

What he'll do is
Boy-calves flinch. Turpentine on balls is like vinegar on an apple. Bitter in their nostrils, a sting on their private parts. He, the chef, brushes turpentine on with a pastry brush until they're basted, ready for the time of fattened meat on their hind quarters. Their halves and their wholes. Turpentine stings my nostrils as the poor thing, we call it, us girls, the poor thing bucks, a would-be bull being frocked. He makes the cut and the babes bellow their way into sexless with an unbroken voice, udderless castratoes. Because my husband knows that this is a man's land and on a man's land there can only be one bull.

What I see is
I look at them and I see – meat.

When I'm big with child I'll hang from the bedhead like a carcass, but for now I'm flat on my back. On the flat of my belly I feel the furry earth of his midriff press its small abrasions into skin that smells of lavender. He smells of raw meat and turd. He smells of toy soldiers. Slouch hats and sweat. He won't wash history off his skin. In bed he'll rub it into

lavender and together we'll make flowers and fields alike,
together we'll make earth and air. We'll be trodden by hard
boots. We'll be fenced and dammed.

What he hates is
Broken cycles. February coming before January. Pumpkins
coming before tomatoes. Hay-baling before shearing, after-
noon before morning, death before life. What he hates is cold
Summers and dry Springs. He knows that lunch follows break-
fast, that women bleed at the beginning and are pregnant by
the end. What he does is, he turns away from my bleeding
body. Because some meat needs to be cooked. Some meat is
too raw.

Here's what I am
When I bellow too soon there's no darkness to mute the cow-
cry of birth, no darkness to mute the red of blood and he's
right, it's about death this land, it's about babies born without
breath. It's about no babies, belly round like a balloon because
of its childless air, round like the planet but there – don't we
know now that the earth is flat.

I'm dried udders and failed crops.

What pleases me is
He's not home when she drops in. Metal hangs from her lobes.
Not of rusted poles but of powders sifted from creekbeds,
metal made into cages by tiny hammers, birdcage play-things
banging gently against her neck. She smells like something

I could eat and rocks her body sideways on its seat. I place my hand on her belly to feel the baby move and there, on the back of my hand, is the soil I sink my fingers into. This is what I know, when he's out mending fences, how the back of my hand rises and falls with the gently shifting earth inside her.

She smells like something he could eat so I bake her into his afternoons. I cream puff her into the kitchen. I place her on a plate in front of him. I pad him with her flesh until his pants are tight, until his belts are straining, until he belches her up and couldn't fit more of her in if he tried.

When I'm big with child I'll smell like biscuits. I'll dress myself in her body and hang from the bedhead and listen to him snort through his great bull-nostrils.

What he does is
He turns away from the raw meat of my bleeding body and in the morning runs his hands along the sunken belly of an aging cow. He recoils from her milkless udders, examines the dry cavities, the cobwebbed caverns, and declares her too late, even for meat. He takes her away from the milkers. For a day she stands at the other end of the paddock. For a night she listens to the bellowing of birth, and by morning has disappeared behind a veil of truck exhaust and tyre tracks on frost.

What I know is
When her time comes she delivers next door. She delivers at home, and I hear her bellowing out into the night. Bellowing

out like the cows. We wake to howling and roll over and I know her then, her and the sluice of bodies, the before-birth the after-birth, and know also that that's how he can love her, man to beast.

She names her baby after greatgrandfathers. Like she's planting him in the dirt with a corpse. Or bringing the corpse out into the air – a shrub, a sapling, a great big tree. Suddenly our own land is empty and though I look through windows and see forever, when he goes out to milk I follow. And where I expect to fade into haze I find myself still there on the dirt. Surrounded by the rusting metal bones that hold us all together.

Here's what I am
I smell of lavender but when I thaw I bleed into plastic. I bleed onto a polystyrene tray. What I know is that women bleed at the beginning of the cycle and not the end. I've got it all backwards. And that's why I see, when I look into the mirror. Meat.